Touched *by* Kindness

Touched *by* Kindness

True Stories of People Blessed by Compassion

Kim Boyce and
Heidi Hess Saxton

VINE BOOKS

SERVANT PUBLICATIONS
ANN ARBOR, MICHIGAN

© 2001 Kim Boyce and Heidi Hess Saxton

Vine Books is an imprint of Servant Publications especially designed to serve evangelical Christians.

Although the stories are based on real people and events, some names and identifying characteristics have been changed to protect the privacy of those involved.

Published by Servant Publications
P.O. Box 8617
Ann Arbor, Michigan 48107

Cover design: Uttley DouPonce DesignWorks, Sisters, Oregon
Cover illustration: Katherine Lloyd

01 02 03 04 10 9 8 7 6 5 4 3 2

Printed in the United States of America
ISBN 1-56955-180-4

Cataloging-In-Publication Data on file at the Library of Congress.

For my mothers: Sandra Hess and Valerie Saxton;
and my godmother, Susan Tan;
my sisters in life: Chris, Kate, Jennifer,
Barbara, and Terry;
and my sisters by choice: Denise, Elizabeth, Karen,
Katie, Katy, Lilian, and Patty.
Your lives are shining examples of love in action.

Heidi

In memory of Gregg Jampol
(1961–1999).
Your life of selfless dedication to those you loved
was an inspiration to all of us
who were blessed to be your friends.

Kim

Table of Contents

Introduction

This is what the Lord says:
"Let not the wise man boast of his wisdom
* or the strong man boast of his strength*
* or the rich man boast of his riches,*
but let him who boasts boast about this:
* that he understands and knows me,*
that I am the Lord, who exercises kindness,
* justice and uprightness on the earth,*
for in these I delight," says the Lord.

JEREMIAH 9:23-24

The car engine had to work a little harder as we climbed that last icy hill to our destination. Rounding the final bend in the road, I (Heidi) eagerly craned forward to catch my first glimpse of what we had driven nearly 150 miles to see—the setting of many happy childhood memories, Lafayette Federated Church. My entire family had long since moved from New Jersey, but I had returned to spend Christmas with a friend.

I gasped when the church finally came into view. The graceful steeple that had once stretched to the sky had been rudely hacked away, leaving the church looking unkempt and forlorn. (I later learned that the steeple had been transplanted to the church's new location.) We pulled into the parking lot, picked our way across the snow and ice, and cautiously entered the front doors of the sanctuary. Inside, the rich burgundy carpet and draperies had faded to reddish pink. The interior was badly in need of a fresh coat of paint. But I was home again.

The grand piano at the front of the room beckoned. Stripping off my coat, I raced up the center aisle, brushing each of the twenty-three rows of pews as I passed by. Tentatively touching the worn ivory keys of the instrument, I sat down, closed my eyes, and began to play. Note after note, the sacred music echoed through the deserted sanctuary and transported me back nearly twenty years.

In my mind I could hear a Sunday evening hymn-sing in progress. Mr. Casterlin, auctioneer by day and choir director nights and weekends, raised his hand to coax the high notes out of us. About halfway back were the Pfaffs and Castners, the Ormeshers and Bjorks. On the other side of the aisle were my first Sunday school teachers, Bob and Thelma Hess (no relation to me), Mrs. Craig, and Mr. Pinter. Behind them sat old Mr. Fee and the man whose name I could not recall—my family affectionately referred to him as "Mr. Amen-a" because of the emphatic way he warbled the final word of each hymn. Near the back were Bob DeVries and Billy Wilson, who ran the youth group in their spare time. And at the front, Pastor Luthman— a holy man who loved to laugh, and who possessed, along with his wife Susan, an infinite capacity to love the sheep of that flock.

These people will always have a special place in my heart; they were the first who taught me by example what it means to follow Christ. When my sister Chris became sick with cancer, our church family brought us food, drove into New York so my mother would not have to venture to Babies' Hospital alone, and kept my sister Kathy and me while Chris was in the hospital. At the tender age of eight, I accepted Jesus into my heart at the invitation of my Sunday school teacher, Miss Raylene Stevenson.

During my volatile teenage years, Barbara and Alex Ferris provided spiritual ballast, inviting me into their home and making time for me. As I prepared to depart for a year of missionary service in Senegal, West Africa, my church family sacrificed to make the trip possible. Through their kindness, each of them in their own way made Jesus very real to me.

In our day and age, a sense of community is hard to come by. Church attendance is now measured in months, even weeks, rather than decades and generations. The sheer size of many churches makes it easy to get lost in a crowd of nameless faces. More than ever, people crave the closeness of community—but don't know where to find it.

Touched by Kindness is for those who yearn to connect, who long to give to and receive from other people around them a little of God's love. More than a tribute to a bygone era, it is a reminder of the treasures in store for those willing to be a source, a recipient, and a student of God's blessing in unexpected circumstances. In the words of beloved author John Powell, "There is a lot of goodness in this world, and often it is found in unlikely persons and places."

The people you will meet in this book are real. Many of the stories were taken from my experiences both here at home and in other parts of the world: Africa, Poland, Mexico—and southern California, which one might argue is much the same as living in Mexico. My coauthor, Kim, spent hours capturing her own experiences and interviewing celebrities and spokespersons for charitable organizations in order to demonstrate what it means to love from a distance. (Chapters written primarily by me are noted by my initials, H.S., while the initials K.B. indicate the work of Kim Boyce.) In order to give you additional ideas of ways you can touch others through your own acts of kindness, we have interspersed the stories and interviews with some practical sections.

We hope that after reading this book, you too will want to celebrate with us acts of kindness wherever you see them—and the beauty of the human heart that has been touched by Love himself.

—*Heidi Hess Saxton*

Part One

Encouraging Gifts
of Kindness

Marguerite was not the sort of woman most people would consider beautiful. She ran a dingy little greasy spoon down the street from my family's house in Hamburg, New Jersey. Her gray-streaked hair was always pulled back in a net, and her arms jiggled as she flipped eggs and pressed the buttons on her cash register. If you talked to Marguerite, you never quite knew which of her eyes was looking at you—one always wandered a bit, and the other was none too steady. When she came from behind the counter to bus the tables, her legs sported miles and miles of varicose veins that ran from the hem of her pea-soup green uniform to the tops of her orthopedic black shoes.

My family had just moved into the area, and it was my first week at school, where I had started the seventh grade. My sister Chris was about to lose her leg to cancer, and my parents were understandably distracted. One day on my way home from school I paused on the curb outside the diner. Fingering the two quarters I had in my pocket, change from my lunch money, I decided I was not ready to go home just yet. So I wandered into the restaurant and plopped down on one of the high stools at the counter.

Marguerite was the only soul in the place. She brought me a plastic-coated menu and a glass of water. "What can I getcha?"

With relief I saw there was something on the menu I could afford. "A Coke, please."

She plunked a few clear cubes into a glass, poured my drink, and set it in front of me. I took a long swig that burned my throat and made my eyes water. "My name's Marguerite," the large woman said. "What's yours?"

And with that, a friendship was born. I found myself telling

Marguerite not only my name, but all sorts of things I had never told anyone else: how scared I was about my sister, and how hard it was to make friends at this new place. She just listened, nodding understandingly as she refilled my Coke glass. After what seemed like just a few minutes, I looked up at the big black-and-white clock on the wall and saw that nearly an hour had passed.

"Oh, no! It's four o'clock! My mother's gonna kill me!" I plunked a quarter on the table and ran all the way home. I knew I'd be in trouble for taking so long to come home from school, but inside I felt light enough to fly.

The beauty of kindness is found in its simplicity. True kindness depends not so much on heroic sacrifice as the gift of presence, of being sensitive to another person's need.

Several years ago I received a Christmas card from my former neighbors in California, whose two daughters had adopted me as their honorary auntie, "Tia Jaide" (Heidi). Along with the note was a copy of an essay the older girl, Eva, had written for her sophomore English class:

This lady used to live in Apartment Number Three. She let us turn cartwheels across her living room rug. It was fun—and we didn't hurt anything because she had no furniture. My mother says that Tia Jaide must have the patience of a saint.

I have a little sister, Tati, and she has three friends. Our parents make us play outside together unless it rains. It was boring until Tia Jaide moved in. She took us to McDonalds and Busters for ice cream and checkers. She read us stories and showed us photo albums full of pictures of places like Budapest and Boston.

Every day after school we watched for her shiny red car to come up the driveway. We always ran out to meet her when we heard her car pull up. "Can we play at your house?" Some days she was too tired, but when she said yes, we skipped up the steps to her house. She'd let us read to her in English. In school we were learning to read in Spanish, but Tia Jaide always made us read to her in English. If we studied hard, she told us, one day we would go to College. She always made it sound like College was the best place in the world.

"I want to be a teacher, like you," I told Tia Jaide. She smiled when I said that. Mama didn't. She said that if College was so important, why didn't Tia Jaide have a family of her own?

I asked Tia Jaide once why she never married, but she just tickled my chin and said that one day she would slow down enough for a man to catch her. And then she called to Tati and her friends and asked which of us could stand on our heads the longest on her living room rug.

I don't know what happened to Tia Jaide. One day a big truck came and took her things away. And then she came to where we were jumping in the pool and said she was moving far away to work. I wanted her to stay. Who would help us with the hard English words? "Don't cry, Cariña," she said. "You are a smart girl—you can help the others with their reading. That way you can practice being a teacher, even now."

Someday, I want to be like her. I want to wear soft dresses and smell nice and sing pretty songs about Jesus. Most of all, I want a soft carpet in my living room, so that all the little kids in my neighborhood have a place to jump and turn cartwheels.

I could scarcely finish reading. I knew that the kids had enjoyed coming to my house. To be honest, I had enjoyed it as much as they—their laughter had made me forget about my own loneliness awhile. But I had no idea I'd made this kind of impression.

Acts of kindness can be like that. It's not the grand gesture or the well-publicized handout that makes the biggest impression. It's the understated, private, and mutually gratifying exchange of friendship that takes on a life of its own, brightening the horizons of giver and taker alike.

In the story of Rebekah and Abraham's servant (see Genesis 24), it is the kindness of the young woman—rather than her outer beauty or eloquence—that told the servant that he had found God's chosen bride for his master's son, Isaac. Her simple act of kindness refreshed a few parched camels—and encouraged the man who had journeyed a long way to find her.

—*H.S.*

Therefore, as God's chosen people, holy and dearly loved, clothe yourselves with compassion, kindness, humility, gentleness, and patience. Bear with each other and forgive whatever grievances you may have against one another.

COLOSSIANS 3:12-13

One

Mr. Fancher's Roll-Top Desk

Two important things are to have a genuine interest in people and to be kind to them. Kindness, I've discovered, is everything in life.

ISAAC BASHEVIS SINGER

The demands of my father's job had caused our family to move three times in as many years. When I was five, we moved to a little white house in central Jersey. Next door, in the big brown house, lived Mr. Fancher. His only son lived far away and never came to visit. That's what our other neighbor, Mrs. Bigley, told us as she scratched our dog Clancey behind the ears. "It's no wonder, of course—the mean old coot."

I wasn't sure what a "coot" was, but I was pretty sure that meant I didn't want to encounter Mr. Fancher. So I stayed in the backyard by the flowerbed, digging an imaginary garden. Clancey stayed by my side, protecting me from old coots and the occasional caterpillar.

A few days later as I dug in the garden, I heard a door slam. I had never seen Mr. Fancher up close, and stood rooted to the spot, shovel in hand. Slowly he shuffled over, then leaned against the fence. "Hello there, Blue Eyes," he chuckled. His eyes sparkled. He didn't look mean at all.

"'Lo," I managed.

"Diggin' your way to China there, Blue Eyes?" He chuckled at his own joke and shuffled back toward the house, leaving me standing with wonderment in the dirt. Just then I heard another door bang. This time it was my mother. "Heidi! Are you bothering Mr. Fancher? Come away from there!"

Slowly Mr. Fancher turned to face her. "No bother, Ma'am. I have a granddaughter about her age. Don't get to see her much anymore. No, Blue Eyes don't bother me a'tall." With that, he went into the house with a satisfying slap of the screen door.

We became friends, Mr. Fancher and I. He even came to our house for dinner from time to time. Once I asked him what a "coot" was, but my mother just hushed me into the kitchen for more ice.

One day Mr. Fancher saw me playing with Clancey in the backyard, and asked my mother if I could come to his house for a glass of lemonade. After we had settled ourselves, he shuffled to his great roll-top desk and pushed the cover back with a rattle, then reached into one of the cubbies and extracted a stack of pictures. Together we looked at pictures of his family, and remembered the good old days when his wife was alive. He also showed me pictures of his granddaughter, who did look a lot like me. Then he'd sing to me the song he used to sing for her. "Beautiful eyes ... she's got such beautiful eyes..."

The following spring, Mr. Fancher died. He left my father his grand old roll-top. The pictures were gone, but sometimes I used to crawl inside the leg space and breathe deeply the rich scent of old wood, remembering fondly the first man who ever told me I was beautiful.

—*H.S.*

Two

Old Meanie Masters

Gray hair is a crown of splendor;
it is attained by a righteous life.
Better a patient man than a warrior,
A man who controls his temper,
than one who takes a city.

PROVERBS 16:31-32

M iss Masters' tiny white house was down the street from mine, right next to the neighborhood ball field. Her property line was marked by a white picket fence, on which she grew immaculately manicured rosebushes, her pride and joy. From the first bud to the last fall pruning, Miss Masters appeared in her garden every morning wearing a simple cotton print housedress and apron. Every afternoon she was back at work again, clipping, weeding … and waiting for the first errant pop-up of the season.

Miss Masters and the young men of the neighborhood did not exactly belong to a mutual admiration society. "Old Meanie

Masters," they chanted as one of their number tiptoed into the old woman's yard to retrieve a wayward ball. "Look out! Old Meanie'll getcha!" And get them she did. Miss Masters' legs were older and slower than the boys' were, but she had a knack for knowing exactly where each ball would land.

"Those nasty, nasty boys," she'd grumble to her rosebushes as she slowly returned to her house, ball in hand, to add to her sizeable collection of sporting goods. The boys would mutter and go home, too. The game was over. Not even their parents could convince the old lady to return their baseballs. They had lost so many balls in her yard that their parents had resorted to rationing: no more than one a week.

Little Susie shared Miss Masters' opinion of the "nasty" neighborhood boys. They called her "Gimpy Four-Eyes" because she wore glasses and one of her legs was shorter than the other, making her walk with a visible limp. Every day after school she would get off the bus and walk past the ball field to her house. More than anything, she wanted to play. Once she even screwed up her courage and asked to play in the outfield, with the other unwanted girls whose mothers insisted they be allowed to play. But it was hopeless. No one wanted a gimp. So she huddled by the rosebush fence, where no one could see her, and watched dejectedly.

One day a voice broke into her thoughts. "What are *you* doing in my yard?" It was more a demand than a question. Susie looked up to find Miss Masters scowling down at her.

"I'm sorry, Ma'am. I just like to watch from here so they don't see me. I'll die if they make fun of me again. It's bad enough they won't let me play." Susie turned her head so the tears didn't show.

"No sense staying here. You'll catch your death of cold. Go on home, now."

The next day on her way to school Susie glanced over at her hiding spot and saw a flash of white. *My notebook,* she thought, and went over to investigate. When she saw what it was, she smiled and slipped her newfound treasure into her book bag.

That afternoon another foul ball flew into Miss Masters' flowers, and once again the old woman got to it before the boys did. "Go home, you nasty boys!" she yelled. A loud groan rose from the field. It was two outs, bases loaded. Not *now!*

Susie saw her chance. Casually she limped over to the captain. "Can I play?"

"Go away, stupid. Game's over. Old Meanie Masters got our ball again!"

"I ... I have a ball."

"YOU! Where'd you get it?!"

"I found it. Can I play?"

"In the outfield. Go on." Scarcely believing her luck, Susie tossed the ball to the pitcher and ran breathlessly to the outfield.

The next morning, another ball was waiting to be plucked from Miss Masters' rosebushes. And like the loaves and fishes, the supply did not dwindle so long as there was a need.

—H.S.

"Happiness is not a station at which to arrive, but a manner for traveling."

MARGARET LEE RUNBECK

"The quality of a person's life is in direct proportion to his commitment to excellence, regardless of his chosen field of endeavor."

VINCE LOMBARDI

Three

Never Too Old to Care

Perhaps you are an older adult who feels alienated from the rest of the world. Maybe a health condition forces you to stay in when you would rather be out and about. Please don't give up! There is something that everyone can do to reach out to others in need.

- Call a friend or relative and encourage them.
- Contribute financially to a ministry you believe in and trust.
- Write a letter to someone who needs to know that you care.
- If your health is good or if you have the gumption to be active in spite of your health, get involved at your church.
- Join a Bible study; your wisdom from living a long life is needed by those younger and less experienced.
- Volunteer to help out at the church office or the local hospital.
- Bake cookies and take them to a frazzled mom with several little ones at home.
- Volunteer in the church nursery and enjoy the warmth of holding a baby.

Remember that what you do is not as important as just doing something. You will be blessed and you will also be a blessing and inspiration to others!

Four

Tale of a Polish Outhouse

*Love each other deeply, because love covers over a multitude of
sins. Offer hospitality to one another without grumbling.*

1 PETER 4:8-9

For some people, "music ministry" conjures up images of big
hair and sequins. For others, it's long hair and acoustic gui-
tars. Me—I think of outhouses. Well, one particular outhouse
situated in the beautiful rolling hills of southwestern Poland.

A group of us were touring by bus across the south of Poland
on a summer outreach team. While parts of the trip had been
very exciting, overall it had been a long summer. Put nearly
thirty people on a bus (plus luggage, sound equipment, and
enough bottled water to float a small yacht), add a couple of
language barriers and several short-lived romantic crushes, and
things are bound to get interesting.

By the end of the third week, I was ready for a break. So
imagine my delight when during a break in rehearsal, a plump-
cheeked Polish matron came up to me and exclaimed, "Good

news! Tonight you will be staying at the mayor's house! He has a beautiful home just outside of town. You can choose five of your team members to join you!"

Excitedly I took a few of my more cooperative team members aside and gave them the news. After the concert, we piled into the mayor's van with visions of fresh sheets and ice cubes dancing in our heads.

About twenty minutes later we pulled up outside a large farmhouse. A small structure stood in the middle of the garden on the side of the house. "Maybe it's the toolshed," offered one woman rather helplessly. Our noses told us otherwise. So did the bird-size mosquitoes that danced through the crescent on the front door of the little shack.

Our host turned to us and pointed out the obvious. "Here are the facilities. Come, let me show you to your room so you can rest before dinner."

All six of us trailed the mayor into the house, where we were greeted enthusiastically by his diminutive wife. "We're so glad you're here! Come in! Come in! Here is your room..." Throwing open the door, she beamed at us happily. "You will be quite comfortable here, I think."

Inside was a queen-sized bed covered with a beautiful hand-made quilt and tons of fluffy pillows. One bed. I looked around for other beds, or a cot or two. Nothing. *Surely there must be some mistake...*

The mayor's wife continued, "The sink is down the hall just off the kitchen if you want to wash up." And with that, she was gone.

At dinner the group was more subdued than usual. The mayor's wife tried to cheer us up with more warm tea (no ice cubes in sight). We refused the extra tea, of course. We all knew what was in store for anyone who overindulged: a midnight rendezvous with the mosquitoes.

The tea hit about an hour later, after we were all settled in bed, three at the foot, three at the head. I was against the wall. It had just gotten quiet when the woman next to me squirmed. "Oh, no…" she whispered.

I had been thinking the same thing. "Me, too," I whispered back.

"What are we gonna *do*?! Those mosquitoes will eat us alive! And they didn't even give us a flashlight!"

I thought for a minute. "Well, there was that little washroom just off the kitchen…"

"You mean—no, I couldn't!"

"Got any better ideas?"

She was quiet. "Well…"

"Come on. I'll go with you."

We crawled over the others and made our way in the dark to the washroom. Inside was a tub and a sink. I pushed the other girl inside. "You go first. I'll keep watch."

She had no sooner closed the door than Mrs. Mayor padded down the stairs. Turning on the light, she seemed startled to see me standing there. "You want I make you some tea?" she offered.

"NO! I mean, I'm waiting for my friend to … brush her teeth."

The sound of running water on metal echoed from the next room. "Your friend brushes her teeth?" She looked at me skeptically.

"I really don't know…" I hedged. Just then the door opened

and my co-conspirator took one look at the mayor's wife and bolted for the bedroom.

I squirmed, but there was no escape. "Come," my hostess patted a kitchen chair. "I make you tea."

—H.S.

Five

Loving Brother, Loyal Friend

We ourselves feel that what we are doing is just a drop in the ocean. But the ocean would be less because of that missing drop.
MOTHER TERESA OF CALCUTTA

M y husband, Gary, had taken our son to McDonalds, and I couldn't reach him. Not knowing what else to do, I picked up the phone and called our friend Gregg. "I'm at the hospital," I told him breathlessly. "I came in for a checkup and I just found out I'm going to have this baby in a couple of hours! Could you come here, get my house key, and then go to our house and get the camera and video camera so we'll be able to document the baby's birth?"

There was a brief pause on the other end of the line. "Of course," Gregg said. "I'll be there in a minute."

He got the equipment and made it back to the hospital in time to encourage my husband and me during the labor process, tell a few jokes to ease our tension, and help baby-sit our three-year-old son while his little brother was being born. I had never been so thankful for our wonderful friend ... and his cellular phone!

It wasn't the only time Gregg was there when we needed him. Many times I enlisted our friend's help when I hit a snag in making flight reservations. "What's your flight number?" he would ask. Then, "I'll call you right back." In a few minutes the phone would ring. "Do you have a pen?" he'd ask me. "Here's your new reservation number. Oh, and by the way, they're not going to charge the $75 change fee."

"How do you do it?" I would ask.

"It's a gift, babe," he would answer jokingly.

Gregg Jampol loved to tell jokes, especially if they were about anything Jewish. He got most of his jokes from his Jewish father, a successful businessman whom Gregg idolized. A brilliant man, Gregg could figure out anything, fix anything, and love anyone.

Although he made his living as a recording engineer working on albums for artists such as BeBe Winans, dc talk, Lari White, and others, Gregg also traveled with Gary and me on the road for five years as our sound technician. There was no venue he couldn't make sound like Carnegie Hall.

Gregg made life on the road fun. It didn't matter if we were in Dallas in July or Virginia in February, roasting in 110-degree heat or freezing for four days on a bus with no heat, he was happy and content. His enthusiasm for life was contagious. He made us laugh. He made our boys laugh.

He was part of our family.

When Gregg died suddenly and unexpectedly at the age of thirty-seven, five hundred people came to his memorial service to mourn his death and celebrate his life.

Gary and I were blessed to have called this man our dearest friend. I want to become more like the kind of person he was ... loving, loyal, compassionate, and a friend to all.

While Gregg's life taught me to be a better friend, it took his death to remind me not to take such friendships for granted. Do you have a friend like Gregg? Take a moment today to call that person, or write a note to let him or her know how your life is richer because of that friendship. Who knows when you'll get another opportunity?

—K.B.

Six

Bus Ride Through Mexico

If I rise on the wings of the dawn,
if I settle on the far side of the sea,
even there your hand will guide me,
your right hand will hold me fast.

PSALM 139:9-10

There are times in life when you realize that maintaining the status quo is highly overrated. In your heart of hearts, you know that you can't stay where you are—and yet, you don't really know where else to go.

It was January, 1991. I had completed my missionary training at Bethany College of Missions (Bloomington, Minnesota) and had spent two years working on campus as a "post-grad." For me at least, the term signified that I had completed my Bible studies but had yet to figure out what to do with my life.

Yet another winter of mind-numbing cold had settled on the city. Snow drifted above the windowpanes. The sky was the color of day-old oatmeal. People were cranky. And I was ready for a change. Any change.

Then, miracle of miracles, two missionary friends invited me to come visit them in Mexico. *Two weeks of nothing but sunshine,* I thought. I decided to take the red-eye to Acapulco and then bus to Michael and Karen's in the northeastern province of San Luis Potosí. I bought my ticket with visions of mariachi bands dancing in my head, and with the hope that while I was on this trip, God would enlighten me about what I was supposed to do next.

A few days later I stepped off the plane in Acapulco expectantly—and was besieged by a swarm of pushing and shoving tourists, ugly Americans growing uglier by the minute. They screamed at the locals like banshees, apparently under the impression that Mexicans will miraculously comprehend English if it is spoken loudly enough. Tourist children ran amok by day. Tourist teens swilled margaritas by night. It was Las Vegas with salsa. I pored over bus schedules and longed for the local color of "real" Mexico.

The next morning, armed with a Spanish dictionary to supplement the five phrases I already knew by heart, a roll of toilet paper (just in case), and a bag of apples, I boarded the bus for Mexico City. There were two seats available—one in the middle of the bus, near a heckling section of Mexican good old boys; and one near the front, beside an elderly *consuela* clad head to toe in black.

Ignoring the catcalls, I sat next to the old woman, who smiled at me kindly. She was my own bit of insurance. I later discovered that sitting with children worked too—in the Mexican culture, mothers wear an invisible badge of respect.

I opened my rucksack and extracted two apples, one for me and one for my seatmate, Señora Martinez. Then I settled back to stare out the window as the road whizzed by at an alarming rate.

I had no sooner settled in than an urchin with a black shock of hair and a brilliant smile popped up from the seat ahead. *"Hola!"*

With a torrent of giggles, his head disappeared once again. He seemed a little old for peek-a-boo, but this was going to be a long bus ride. It wouldn't hurt to make a new friend.

Just then there was a scuffling sound in the seat in front of Señora Martinez. Another dark head popped up. *"Hola!"*

He, too, disappeared and then bounced into view again. *"Me llamo Pedro!"*

This time the old lady chuckled. I reached back into my sack and pulled out two more apples, holding them above the seats in front of me. Two grubby little hands snatched them from my grasp. More giggles.

I had two new friends.

Across the aisle sat a dark-eyed youth. Martin had a rudimentary grasp of English—marginally better than my Spanish. He pointed out the little shrines along the winding, treacherous roads. *"Eez where karkresh."*

I looked at him blankly. Martin made a whistling sound in the gap between his front teeth and pantomimed a car going over an embankment. *"Karkresh."*

Lovely. I gritted my teeth and willed the wheels to the road.

As evening approached we stopped at a small village for dinner. As luck would have it, it was festival time. Beautiful young ladies clad in miles of satin and ribbon twirled and swayed to

Mexican folk music. I bought a brightly colored serape for myself, two paper sombreros for Pedro and his friend Jose, and an ice for Señora Martinez.

The señora continued to look after me for the rest of the evening, shooing away with a scowl and a clucking sound the local men who seemed intrigued by the fact that I was traveling alone.

At the designated time—give or take twenty minutes, which I learned to expect in Mexico—we got back on the bus and drove through the night. The advantage of nighttime driving, I discovered, was that I couldn't see the hairpin turns in the road.

Martin had disappeared, but Pedro and Jose provided a welcome distraction. They seemed ridiculously pleased with their new hats, although I didn't understand a word they were chortling in their excitement. When they finally calmed down enough to realize that I didn't speak their language, they good-naturedly tried to teach me. *"Uno ... dos ... tres,"* intoned Pedro, holding up his fingers. I repeated the words solemnly, then smiled and held up *my* fingers. "One ... two ... three." They giggled and dived back into their seat.

The next morning when we arrived in Matehuala, I thanked Señora Martinez for her kindness. I had approached her on that stifling, crowded bus as a stranger—as a single young woman traveling alone, I must have given her some cause for suspicion. Still, she took me in. Language barriers had precluded the simplest conversation between us. And yet, her gift of presence enabled me to experience her country not as a tourist but as a guest.

—*H.S.*

Seven

The Sisters of Real de Catorce

It is not lost time to wait on God.

HUDSON TAYLOR

I had been in Mexico just a few days, visiting with my missionary friends Michael and Karen Leeming, when we decided to take a day excursion to the old silver mining town, Villa Real de Nuestra Señora de la Concepción de Guadalupe de los Alamos de los Catorce—or "Real de Catorce," as the locals called it. Most of the silver had long since been stripped from the hills, but the town was still a popular site for tourists.

I had come to Mexico to get some perspective about my future, removing myself from the daily routine of my work in Minneapolis for a few weeks in order to hear God's voice more clearly. So far I had not accomplished much except to unwind a bit, and had not heard anything more remarkable than the occasional lizard slithering under the brush. But I figured God would clue me in when he was ready.

The town could be reached only through a dark tunnel a mile long and only one car wide. Roadside shrines, by now familiar sights, dotted the underground route, with each shrine holding a single candle in memory of one of the many who had died during the tunnel excavation years before.

Real de Catorce is dominated by the Cathedral of San Francesco. The church contains a life-sized statue of their patron, Francis of Assisi. After we climbed the steps of the church, we passed a group of nuns who looked very tired and hot, clad in gray habits and white wimples. Silently they knelt to pray. As I watched, every trace of fatigue disappeared from their faces as they drew within themselves to meet with their beloved Spouse. I tiptoed away, hoping they had not noticed me, and feeling a little embarrassed for having intruded on such a holy moment.

I saw the sisters again as I made my way among the vendors, looking for silver bracelets to take back home as gifts. As they passed me, I was surprised to hear them speaking to one another in English. "Oh, could we? But we just had ice cream yesterday. It would be such an extravagance..."

Stopping beside a pushcart loaded with fruit-flavored ices, the tallest sister peered doubtfully inside. "We really shouldn't. Such a waste of money."

I stepped up. "Please, sisters. Allow me to treat you." The nuns looked at me with surprise, and then turned to the tall sister for her decision. Thoughtfully she regarded me. "You were at the church just now, were you not?"

"Yes, that was me," I admitted.

But there was no reproach in her voice, only compassion. "I thought so. I prayed for you. You were sitting there all alone, watching us, and it seemed right to ask God to help you."

"Thank you. Actually, that's partly why I'm here. I need to decide what to do next, whether to return to college—or do something else."

"We will continue to pray. In the meantime—yes, I think a lemon ice would be very nice." And in a short time, lemon ices had been passed all around.

All too soon my vacation was over, and I boarded my plane back to Minneapolis. At home, two pieces of mail caught my attention. One was a postcard from the sisters, thanking me again for the ices. The other was a catalog from Azusa Pacific University. I had heard from fellow classmates that APU accepted up to two years of class credits from Bethany graduates. I had contemplated going back to school, but after four years of Bible training I wasn't sure this was what God had in mind. Now, holding the catalog in my hands, I remembered the sister's promise to pray, and recognized that this was God's answer. I knew I was California-bound.

—H.S.

Eight

"Stupid, but not Dishonest"

> *Do all the good you can,*
> *In all the ways you can,*
> *In all the places you can,*
> *At all the times you can,*
> *To all the people you can,*
> *As long as ever you can.*
>
> JOHN WESLEY

In the fall of 1991 I entered Azusa Pacific College, a small Christian liberal arts college in southern California. The warm climate and casual atmosphere soon worked their magic on me, but by springtime I was ready for another adventure.

When an advertisement appeared on a student bulletin board asking students to join one of several summer missions teams that would be performing outdoor concerts throughout Russia, Hungary, and Poland that summer, I eagerly applied. To my surprise, I was asked to lead one of the teams. Although others on the team had more musical ability, I was several years older than most students and had lived abroad.

Seven American students, including six from my school, had been accepted on the same team. We were all very excited about having the chance to share God's love with people in Eastern Europe, and right away we started praying for those we would meet along the way. As the date of our departure drew closer, we were told that we would fly to Frankfurt, then travel by train to Budapest, where we would meet the other twenty people on our team for music rehearsal.

One of my first tasks as leader was to get the seven of us safely to Budapest. Shortly before our trip I was given the plane tickets and train passes. The latter consisted of a white sheet of paper and six little sticks of cardboard. "Those must be the group tickets," someone explained to me.

We arrived in Frankfurt without incident, and the next morning we found our seats on the train. I smiled at an old man across the aisle from us; he was traveling with a little boy.

"Opa!" The child pulled on the old man's sleeve and showed him something in his book. Opa... grandfather. I smiled. My high-school German would come in handy.

We had barely pulled out of the station when the conductor made his way up the aisles to collect tickets and check papers. When he arrived at our seats, I handed him our passports along with the white sheet of paper and the cardboard stubs.

"Wo ist ihren Karte?" the conductor asked. Our tickets? I was not sure I had heard him correctly. Why was he asking for tickets when they were in his hand?

Pointing to his hand, I replied, *"Hier."*

"Sind nicht Karten," he replied, irritated. Clearly there was only one explanation for my stupidity. *"Americanische?"*

"Yes, we're American," I admitted.

He sighed heavily, then jerked his head toward the front of the car. "Bring your passports and come with me."

"What's going on?" the others wanted to know.

"Something's wrong with our tickets. Pray!" I hissed back. I followed the conductor to the car at the far end of the train, where six large German men were stuffed like sausages inside the compartment. Seeing us, they squeezed together even more so I could wedge between two of them.

Animated conversation filled the air like machine gun fire. From time to time the man next to me would lean over and chide, "You have BEEG problem. BEEG problem." His breath smelled like sauerkraut. I hadn't a clue what they were saying, or what I would do if they threw us off the train. Mentally I checked off my options. We did not have enough money among us to pay for another set of tickets, and I had no way to contact the leader until we arrived in Budapest.

I decided I'd better cast myself on their mercy. *"Bitte* ... please. We are American missionaries on our way to Budapest. We have no money. I was told that this"— I pointed to the paper in my captor's hands— "was all we needed to get on the train. Our leader will meet our train in Budapest. He can explain everything."

Another staccato exchange. More doubtful, sidelong looks. At last it was decided that I would pay them $50 as good-faith money, which would be refunded at the Frankfurt office as soon as the tickets were produced. The conductor scribbled something on my ticket and gave me back our passports. With shaking knees I wobbled back to my seat.

I had just finished explaining what had happened to the group when we reached the Austrian border. The German conductor got off the train, the Austrian conductor got on the train. This one was skinny, with red hair sticking out from under his cap. He reached my seat and held out his hand for my ticket. Somehow I knew what was coming next.

"Where is your ticket? You are Americans, yes?"

"Yes. The German conductor said we could ride to Budapest with this. See? He signed it here."

"It does not say you can go to Budapest. This was only good for Germany…" He stood back and studied me for a moment. Something about his expression made me want to take a bath. He reached out and touched my cheek. "But I like you, so you can stay."

I wanted to clobber him, but figured I'd better not push my luck. "Thank you," I managed, looking away. The old man across the aisle smiled sympathetically at me.

We rode without incident until we reached the edge of Austria. Then the Austrian conductor got off the train and the Hungarian conductor got on … followed by the Hungarian police. The police started checking papers on one end of the train as the Hungarian conductor began to check tickets from the other end. You can guess where the two groups met. The Hungarian policeman demanded our passports just as the conductor was saying, "But where are your tickets? This is not a ticket!"

Nuts. I was going to spend the rest of my summer in a Hungarian prison, singing with the other team members, just like Paul and Silas.

As I started to explain, "Opa" interrupted me. He explained to the officials that we had been hassled ever since we got on the train in Frankfurt. "They are stupid, but not dishonest. Let them go," the old man concluded. Figuring dim-witted was easier to live with than incarcerated, I gave the conductor my best innocent smile.

The policeman sighed and scribbled something in our passports, then handed them back. The conductor scribbled something on the ticket and handed it back. Once they had safely passed our seats, I caught the old man's eye. *"Danke, Opa."* He winked at me, then went back to entertaining his grandson.

We had been on the road only a day, and already God had found a way to remind us of his love through this kindly old man. I closed my eyes and leaned back in my seat. It was going to be a great trip.

—H.S.

Nine

The Bordello-Red Sofa

The rich man is not one who is in possession of much, but one who gives much.

JOHN CHRYSOSTOM

The California breezes wafted through my living room window, rustling the vertical blinds that shielded me from the cold, hard realities outside my little oasis. I had finished my college studies the previous year, and now I was on my own, having secured my first job that paid well enough for me to get my own apartment.

Of course, a glorified secretary's salary doesn't stretch very far in southern California, and so I was living in what would politely be called a "colorful" section of a Los Angeles suburb south of Pasadena. The mariachi garage band in the apartment complex behind mine played till the wee hours of the morning, and small, tan children jumped in and out of the pool, shouting in Spanish at the top of their lungs. I was the only Caucasian in the whole complex, and I think my neighbors felt compelled to look out for the crazy single lady in *Apartmento Tres.*

It started the first day I moved in. I had just unpacked all my worldly possessions—a few boxes of kitchen utensils and books—and sprawled for a good read on my brand-new corn-flower-blue carpet when the welcome wagon appeared. Tatiana was about eight years old with big brown eyes and scrawny brown legs, her hair tied back in long ponytails.

"Buena dias…. Whatcha doin'?"

I set my book aside and chided myself for leaving the front door open. *"Nada."*

Tatiana's older sister Eva surveyed the broad expanse of bare carpet judiciously. "Can we play?"

I stood up, gradually warming to the idea of having company. "Who wants a cookie?"

That did it. I had five friends for life. We had nearly polished off the batch I had baked that afternoon when one of the mothers showed up. "What are you kids doing here? I'm sorry they bother you, Señorita."

"Oh, no bother. I was getting a little lonely. Have a cookie."

The woman chewed slowly as she regarded my living room. "Your furniture no arrived yet?"

I nodded. "I'm going through a minimalist phase right now." She looked at me blankly. "It's all here," I added.

Miscomprehension turned to puzzlement. "This is *it?*"

"Pero, Mama!" Tatiana protested. "We can turn *cartwheels!* And we no bump anyting!"

Her mother had an expression in her eyes I could not quite decipher. A little sadness, perhaps. Or pity.

After that there was some token of friendship on my doorstep several times each week … a few oranges, a plate of *empanadas* (tasty little meat pies). At first I felt like the neighborhood charity case, and was sorry I had not made it clear to Tatiana's mother that I *liked* living this way, without even a sofa. In a short time, however, I realized that my neighbors' generosity was prompted not by my lack of furniture, but by the fact that I had opened my heart to their little girls. I was miles from home—but to these people, I was family.

Over the next few months, my life developed a comfortable routine. I would come home from work to find five girls perched like little vultures on my stoop. At the first sight of me they would jump up and down. "Tia Jaide! Tia Jaide!" Then we would go inside for cookies and English reading lessons. When it was time for supper, the girls would go home, and I would lock my door and prepare to spend a quiet evening at home. There was no way I'd open my door after dark in that neighborhood.

Then one night around 9:00 I heard a lot of shuffling outside, followed by loud and angry male exclamations. A knock came at my door. Surprised and a little apprehensive, I peeked through the vertical blind.

Five large men were standing on my front porch, surrounding a large object. The light wasn't very good, and I couldn't tell what it was. Nor did I recognize any of the men. "Who is it?" I called, stalling.

An impatient voice wrangled its way through the blind. "It's Tatiana's father. Open *la puerta*."

I put on the chain and opened the door a crack. "Yes?"

"My kids, they say you have no furniture. You want this?"

I glanced down. The love seat was covered in a ghastly red brocade—*bordello red*, I thought. A nondescript stain was

53

emblazoned on one of the cushions. A bold fashion statement, to be sure ... but I didn't have the heart to have them carry it back down three flights of stairs.

"Come on in," I said.

It is more blessed to give than to receive (Acts 20:35).

—H.S.

Ten

Twenty-Five Easy Ways
to Be a Kind Neighbor

1. *Introduce yourself.* Greeting your neighbors (and their children) by name is the first step in building community.
2. *Don't give your neighbors a reason to grumble.* Keep your lawn neat and litter-free. If you have pets, clean up after them. If you have children, watch to be sure they don't invade your neighbor's space.
3. *When possible, practice tolerance.* Is it really that big a deal if your neighbor's dog chases a squirrel into your yard? Resist the temptation to let things come before people.
4. *Share the bounty.* If you're making meals for that week or doing some baking, make a little extra for a busy mother or single person.
5. *Notice things.* Admire the new geraniums in their yard, or the "A" on little Jimmy's school paper.
6. *Celebrate occasions big and small.* Leave a small flowering plant on the doorstep on the first day of spring, a balloon (perhaps with a string tied around a candy bar) for a child's birthday.

Is your neighbor single?

7. Invite him or her for dinner occasionally–just because you recognize cooking for one can be a hassle.

8. If your neighbor lives far from family, invite him or her to join you for some holiday meals or family outings.

9. If your church is having a special outreach to singles, invite your neighbor and offer to go with him or her.

10. Notice something he or she does well, and offer a sincere compliment—ask for a recipe, or advice about buying a computer or fixing a toaster. Let your neighbor know that you value the friendship.

11. If your single neighbor seems to like kids, have your children draw (and deliver) pictures for him or her.

12. Fly a kite! On a warm spring weekend, take your kids to the local park to fly a kite—and ask your neighbor if he or she would like to come along. Don't forget to go for ice cream afterward.

13. Does your neighbor have a pet? Offer to take care of your neighbor's "baby" when he or she goes away on vacation or a business trip.

14. Do you know someone who might be a good match for your single neighbor? Invite them both to an informal dinner or barbecue with a few other friends—and let things take their course without any pressure or expectation.

Is your neighbor a young parent?

15. If you're going to the grocery store, ask if she needs anything—save her the hassle of going!

16. If a new baby is added to the family, pay a little extra attention to the other children. They need a little TLC right now.

17. Those new parents might also appreciate your bringing dinner over for the family a few times during those first tough weeks.

18. Is your neighbor a single parent? Encourage him or her as often as you can. Watch for ways to serve that family in practical ways.

19. Do you share a laundry room? See if your neighbor needs a load run while yours is in the dryer.

20. Are the dark circles around her eyes getting darker every day? Offer to sit with the kids in a "safe place" such as their living room (or in yours, if the baby is fussy) for an hour so she can take a nap.

21. Invite the older children to your house to bake cookies. (If you're not Betty Crocker, cut the cookies out of a tube and let the kids go wild with sprinkles!)

Are your neighbors sick or elderly?

22. Check in at least once each day, just to see if they need anything.

23. Take over a basket with a few slices of cake, a pretty teapot, and a teacup for everyone. Ask if they have time for a cup of "friendship tea."

24. Offer to go to the drugstore, or take them to a doctor's appointment if they need a ride.

25. If your neighbors are homebound, offer to take them to church with you on Sundays. If they are too sick to travel, ask if they'd like a visit from a pastor—then follow up! (Note: If your neighbors come from a different denomination than you do, offer to contact their church to alert them to your neighbors' need.)

Part Two

The Life-Giving Way
of Compassion

For he will deliver the needy who cry out,
the afflicted who have no one to help.
He will take pity on the weak and the needy
and save the needy from death.

I n *Abba's Child,* Brennan Manning describes the time he
and his wife Rosalyn encountered a young woman in the
French Quarter of New Orleans. Susan was soliciting
donations for the Unification Church. Brennan writes:

Obviously she had two strikes against her. First, she was a
pagan and did not acknowledge Jesus Christ as her Lord and
Savior. Second, she was a mindless, witless, naïve and vulner-
able kid who had been brainwashed by a guru and mesmer-
ized by a cult.

"You know something, Susan?" I said. "I deeply admire
your integrity and your fidelity to your conscience. You're
out here tramping the streets doing what you really believe
in. You are a challenge to anyone who claims the name
'Christian.'"

Roslyn reached out and embraced her, and I embraced the
two of them.

"Are you Christians?" she asked.

Rosalyn said, "Yes."

She lowered her head and we saw tears falling on the sidewalk. A minute later she said, "I've been on my mission here
in the Quarter for eight days now. You're the first Christians
who have been nice to me. The others have either looked at
me with contempt or screamed and told me I was possessed
by a demon. One woman hit me with her Bible."

What makes the Kingdom come is heartfelt compassion: a
way of tenderness that knows no frontiers, no labels, no com-
partmentalizing, and no sectarian divisions. Jesus, the human
Face of God, invites us to deep reflection on the nature of
true discipleship and the radical lifestyle of Abba's child.

Brennan Manning, *Abba's Child* (Colorado Springs: NavPress, 1994) 76-77.

Compassion differs from simple kindness not so much by the nature of our actions but by its fruit—both in us and in the object of our compassion. Mercy's "kissing cousin," compassion is an ongoing expression of the life that God pours into us. While kindness encourages, compassion gives life, whether that life is spiritual, emotional, or physical.

My favorite image of the compassion of Christ is found in the eighth chapter of John, the story of the woman caught in adultery who was dragged before Jesus. The Pharisees, breathing murderous rage, flung her on the ground before him and demanded that he pronounce her sentence.

Put yourself in the woman's shoes for a moment. Your darkest secret exposed, you have been tossed to the ground, mortified and utterly alone, at Jesus' feet. You dare not look up, and wonder if the stones will hurt very much when they start to pelt your body like hail.

By Law, you are condemned, no matter how much you beg or what the circumstances of your wrongdoing might be. In a daze you wait for the sentence to be carried out … and the next thing you know, you are being helped to your feet by a man who looks at you with an expression of tender love that takes your breath away. You can hardly meet his gaze—yet you know at that moment that your life will never be the same.

Jesus' treatment of the woman caught in adultery is the essence of compassion. Those who are touched by such compassion—whether as giver or receiver—find new life.

This section contains examples of life-giving compassion. As you read, consider what opportunities God might be bringing your way—opportunities to enrich your life as you touch the lives of others in desperate need of compassion.—*H.S.*

Eleven

Chocolate Cake Mystery

So [Elijah] went to Zarephath. When he came to the town gate, a widow was there gathering sticks. He called to her and asked, "Would you bring me a little water in a jar so I may have a drink?" As she was going to get it, he called, "And bring me, please, a piece of bread."

"As surely as the Lord your God lives," she replied, "I don't have any bread—only a handful of flour in a jar and a little oil in a jug. I am gathering a few sticks to take home and make a meal for myself and my son, that we may eat it—and die."

Elijah said to her, "Don't be afraid. Go home and do as you have said. But first make a small cake of bread for me ... from what you have and bring it to me, and then make something for yourself and your son. For this is what the Lord, the God of Israel, says: 'The jar of flour will not be used up and the jug of oil will not run dry until the day the Lord gives rain on the land.'"

She went away and did as Elijah had told her. So there was food every day for Elijah and for the woman and her family.

1 KINGS 17:10-15

It had been a rough winter. My ten-year-old sister Chris had lost her leg in her long battle with cancer. As the bills continued to pile up, the belt my parents had drawn tighter and tighter around our family finances had left us all more than a little winded.

The summer of my sophomore year in high school, things got a little brighter. I had always wanted to be an exchange student. As a concession to my wanderlust, my parents agreed to host a student that year. Jaana was from Finland—a junior, blue-eyed, blonde, and beautiful enough to make even the senior boys swoon. I enjoyed the novelty of having a Finnish friend, and especially liked that at last I had an identity I could live with. I was no longer the four-eyed Christian geek who didn't wear makeup or cool clothes. I was Jaana's little sister.

That winter, Jaana's parents wrote to tell us that they were hoping to visit America at Easter, and my parents immediately wrote back to invite them to stay with us.

Then tragedy struck. One month before Jaana's parents were to arrive, Chris wound up back in the hospital for another operation that sucked the family bank account drier than last week's soup bone.

The week before our guests arrived, I overheard my parents talking one night when they thought everyone was asleep. What were we going to do? How would we feed our guests? Should we find another place for Jaana to stay? Not wanting to hear the answers to those questions, I covered my ears with my pillow and went to sleep with an uneasy gnawing in the pit of my stomach.

The next morning as we sat down to our traditional Sunday morning donuts, Dad announced that we were going to ask

God to help us. "You will NOT ask anyone at church for help," Dad reminded us. "They've done enough." Then he bowed his head and implored Almighty God to do something.

Three hours later, when we returned from church, we discovered that someone had propped open our front porch door. Dad ordered us to stay in the car until he made sure everything was all right. The next thing we heard was the sound of my father's deep, booming laugh.

On the porch, just to the right of the door, sat ten large boxes of food—enough to feed us for months. And on top of the largest box was the biggest miracle of all: a huge, delectable, three-layered chocolate cake—my favorite. There was no note, and everyone who heard the story looked as surprised as we had been.

"God must have sent his angels to take care of us," my mother said later that evening. My dad just nodded, took a sip of tea, and buried his nose back in the newspaper. That special delivery from God's compassionate angel (whoever it was) did more than feed our bodies. It fed our souls with the reassurance that God loved us and had not forgotten us—and that as long as we trusted him, we would always have a little left over for the stranger at our door.

—H.S.

Twelve

The Eight Degrees of Charity

The first and lowest degree is to give, but with reluctance or regret. This is the gift of the hand, but not the heart.

The second degree is to give cheerfully, but not in proportion to the distress of the sufferer.

The third degree is to give cheerfully and in proportion to the suffering, but not until the gift is solicited.

The fourth degree is to give cheerfully, proportionally and even unsolicited, but to put it in the poor man's hand, thereby shaming him.

The fifth degree is to give charity in such a way that the distressed may receive the bounty, and know their benefactor without being known by him.

The sixth degree is to know the objects of one's bounty, but to remain unknown to them.

The seventh degree is still more meritorious, namely to bestow charity in such a way that the benefactor may not know the relieved person, nor they the name of the benefactor.

The eighth degree, and the most meritorious of all, is to anticipate charity by preventing poverty. That is, to assist the reduced fellow man ... by teaching him a trade, or by putting

him in the way of business, so that he may earn an honest liveli-
hood and not be forced to the dreadful alternative of holding
out his hand for charity.

RABBI MOSES BEN MAIMONIDES, A.D. 1135

Thirteen

Bird Feeders, Ice Pops, and Rosemary

Because of the Lord's great love we are not consumed,
for his compassions never fail.
They are new every morning;
great is your faithfulness.

LAMENTATIONS 3:22-23

My mother's friend, whom we called Aunt Rosemary, had kind brown eyes and a gentle voice—in fact, everything about her was gentle. She had three children; her oldest daughter, Hope, was a year younger than me. The eldest in our families, we would sometimes tease our younger siblings, locking them out of the room where we were playing just to hear them scream. Their squeals had a deliciously desperate quality.

Our fun was usually short-lived. Aunt Rosemary would lure the kids out to the kitchen and feed them ice pops and let them sprinkle birdseed in the bird feeder outside, leaving Hope and me to join them or not, as we chose. Usually we chose, reluctantly, to join them.

When I was eleven I overheard Mother tell Daddy that something was wrong with Aunt Rosemary, that she had a disease named after some baseball player... What was it?

"Lou Gehrig's Disease?" inquired my father.

"Yes, that's it! M.L.S.," she replied. This disease cruelly attacks the central nervous system, leaving the mental faculties intact.

Rosemary's condition deteriorated rapidly, and within six months from the time she was diagnosed, she was wheelchair-bound. Within a year, the only voluntary movement she had left was the flickering of her eyelids. She lived this way for years. The isolation must have been terrible for someone so young and vital. Her family "talked" with her through a series of systematic guesses. The alphabet was divided into four parts, with a key word for each: apple (A-E), girl (G-L), manner (M-R), stay (S-Z).

After watching them use this system a few times, I approached the wheelchair. "Hi, Aunt Rosemary. Did you see how tall the corn is growing out in the field next door? Blink once for yes... Good! Yep, knee high by the Fourth of July. Is your family going to do something for the Fourth? Yes? Let me guess ... what does it start with? Apple? Girl? Man ... Manner. Okay. What letter? M? N? O? P.... Okay, the first letter is P. Hmm.... How about the second letter? Apple? Girl? Girl. What letter? G? H? I? I. P-I. A picnic? You're going on a picnic! So's my family..."

My mother visited Aunt Rosemary up to the end, after many others had stopped. Some were uncomfortable carrying on a conversation with someone who couldn't talk back. Others simply had other things clamoring for attention. Sadly, there were also those for whom Rosemary was an uncomfortable reminder that God does not always do what we ask, no matter how hard we pray.

Her daughter and I would sometimes hide in her room, talking in whispers about Aunt Rosemary. It was so unfair, all of it. Her mother was so good and kind. Why was this happening to her, to all of them? My friend never complained about having to take on so much responsibility—getting her brother and sister ready for school, cleaning the house, attending to her mother's most personal needs. The hardest part, she said, was watching her mother die on the outside while her inside was so alive.

I didn't know what to say. At that point in my life, my mother was the last person on earth to whom I would have turned for advice. Instead I watched her tend to Aunt Rosemary—reading to her from her well-marked Bible, scratching her friend's nose when it itched, and baking cookies for her kids when they came home from school.

When I think of the word "compassion," I think first of my mother filling the bird feeder just outside Rosemary's window before coming back inside to wet her friend's lips with a lemon ice pop.

—H.S.

Fourteen

A Knock at the Door

*If you spend yourselves in behalf of the hungry
and satisfy the needs of the oppressed,
then your light will rise in the darkness,
and your night will become like the noonday.*

ISAIAH 58:10

I was upstairs working at the computer when I heard a knock at the front door. My husband answered the knock, and I continued working.

After several minutes, I heard Gary talking to someone about Jesus and wondered who it might be. But I was too preoccupied to get up and check.

Gary walked to the bottom of the stairs and called up to me: "Kim, come down and pick out some magazines you want to buy." I couldn't believe he was going to purchase something we really didn't need from someone we didn't even know!

As I walked into the kitchen, Gary introduced me to the young woman he'd been talking with. "Kim, this is Christy. She's selling magazines to make enough money to pay for legal help to get her little girl back."

"Where is your daughter?" I asked.

"With her father. He stole her," Christy replied, and then we heard the rest of her story.

Christy was eighteen years old. She had been raised by a single mother, who had tried to provide a stable home for her children. She had taken them to church, and Christy had accepted Christ at a young age. But peer pressure and life without a daddy were difficult obstacles for Christy to overcome.

By the time she was fourteen, Christy had become a gang member. They were a violent, even deadly crowd, but the gang provided her with a sense of family. After three years in the gang, however, she realized that if she didn't get out, she wouldn't live to see her twentieth birthday. Her resolve to leave the gang had been strengthened when she found out she was pregnant. Christy knew the gang was no place for a baby. In her efforts to leave, however, she was beaten repeatedly and barely escaped with her life.

During the months that she was pregnant, Christy knew that she had to make some changes in her life. She stopped taking drugs, broke up with her boyfriend, and started going to church again. She rededicated her life to the Lord. She got a job that would help her support her baby. When her daughter was born, Christy knew she would love this little girl forever. Her future began to look brighter.

Then a few days before Christmas, her baby's father had called and asked to take his daughter Christmas shopping. Christy had reluctantly agreed.

She had not seen her little girl since. The agencies that tried to help her sort out her problem said that even though most of their services were free, the legal process of finding her daughter and having her returned would cost money. So Christy had taken the best job she could find—selling magazines door-to-door, ten hours per day, and riding a bus every night with thirty other young adults from different areas of the country who were trying to make a living the same way.

Gary and I were moved by Christy's story. Where would we be if we hadn't had the solid family backgrounds we'd been blessed with? How could we possibly help this young woman? Could our efforts really make a difference in her life?

We did what we could that day to encourage Christy in the direction she was taking her life. We talked with her for two hours. We fixed her dinner and packed a bag of sandwiches, chips, and fruit for her to take with her when she left our house. We grabbed a couple of books off our bookshelves that we thought might help and encourage her and gave them to her as well. And we bought a few magazines.

Yet as Christy walked down our front steps to continue her door-to-door sales, we felt sadly ineffectual. There had to be more we could do. But what? Our only answer was to pray for Christy. And we have. We've prayed for her often and wondered how she's doing, and whether or not she ever got her daughter back. We may never hear from her again, but we did what we could to try to help someone in need.

At times God entrusts us with a single scene in the story of someone's life. In the scope of eternity, our efforts seem miniscule. And yet, God does not measure time—or people—the way we do. Scripture tells us "a thousand years in your sight are like a day that has just gone by, or like a watch in the night" (Ps 90:4).

If we are faithful to the opportunities God sets before us, we can trust him to weave each small act of compassion, each minute of our "watch," into something big enough to make a real difference in the life of someone else.

Only God knows the end of each story. "Teach us to number our days aright, that we may gain a heart of wisdom," the psalmist writes. And later, "May the favor of the Lord our God rest upon us; establish the work of our hands for us—yes, establish the work of our hands" (Ps 90:12, 17).

—*K.B.*

Fifteen

A Church That Cares About the Poor

I have learned to live each day as it comes,
And not to borrow trouble by dreading tomorrow.
It is the dark menace of the future that makes cowards of us.

DOROTHY DIX

*M*y paternal great-grandmother played in a Salvation Army band, and my father served for many years on the board of directors of the Salvation Army in our hometown. Most people know that the Salvation Army is a Christian charity because of the bell ringers who stand outside grocery stores and department stores collecting money in their signature red kettles every holiday season. Most of us are not aware, however, of the magnitude of this organization's work.

Elsie was the daughter of an Italian immigrant and a Kentucky farm girl. Her family was poor and didn't attend church. Elsie sometimes went on her own, but she was embarrassed about her appearance. Even though her clothes were always clean, her hand-me-down dresses were faded, and her discomfort kept her from attending church as often as she would have liked.

Late in her teens, Elsie heard of a church that loved poor people—and the next Sunday she was sitting in a pew at the Salvation Army church. No one stared at her because her dress was old. No one found it strange that she was alone. Finally she had found a place where she felt loved and accepted. Within weeks, Elsie had accepted Jesus Christ as her Savior. A few months later, Elsie's boyfriend, Glenn, had begun to attend church with her, and he too accepted the Lord.

Four years later, Elsie and Glenn were married, the first Christians in both their extended families. Because of Elsie and Glenn's commitment to Christ and their example, their parents and many of their twenty-two siblings became Christians.

The ministry of the Salvation Army in the life of one young girl has affected hundreds of lives. Elsie and Glenn's children, grandchildren, and great-grandchildren have been raised in Christian homes with godly parents.

I know Elsie as Nanny Elsie. She is my husband's grandmother and my little boys' great-grandmother. She and Popaw Glenn are the spiritual backbone of this great family that I now call my own. I will always have a tender place in my heart for the Salvation Army and their mission of reaching out to those in need, and especially for welcoming a poor Italian girl into their church and telling her of a Savior who would always love her ... faded dress and all.

—*K.B.*

Sixteen

Michelle and the Mackewitz Kids

Jesus called the children to him and said, "Let the little children come to me, and do not hinder them, for the kingdom of God belongs to such as these. I tell you the truth, anyone who will not receive the kingdom of God like a little child will never enter it."

LUKE 18:16-17

On a warm summer afternoon, you could smell them two blocks away. The Mackewitz kids. No one ever referred to them individually; they always traveled as a pack. Self-preservation had taught them long ago not to break ranks, and so they went through life in unison, snarling at teachers and beating up small children.

Frankly, I hated them. They tormented me every day on their way to school as they passed my safety guard station; my safety patrol badge irked them the way a matador's red cape riles a bull. But I was afraid of them, so I contented myself with glowering at them from a safe distance once they had passed my station.

Only one kid seemed immune to the Mackewitz kids' meanness. Michelle was in the special-ed class. She had the curves of a young woman and the mind of a child. She spoke in a repetitive singsong that irritated most people. Her words were often liberally peppered with a staccato "he-he-he-he-he."

No one else ever got the joke.

And no one wanted to be around her—not even her parents. Every day after school, Michelle wandered the streets in her tight jeans and low-cut shirts, sometimes until late at night. I felt sorry for her, but I didn't treat her any differently than the others did. I was having enough trouble trying to fit in with the junior high crowd myself. Michelle was a liability I could not afford.

My mother, who didn't understand this delicate balance of nature, ignored my protests and invited Michelle to go along to church with us. She was so hungry for any kind of love that she would have gone with us to the moon, I think. But the kids in Sunday school weren't any nicer than the kids at school, and soon Michelle no longer came around our house when it was time for church.

I'd still see her in school, though. Every day at recess we'd go to our usual places: the Mackewitz kids would congregate at one end of the playground; I read my book on the benches a safe distance away. Michelle would climb onto a swing and beg those nearby to push her. The kind ones got up and walked away. The others usually hassled her until she cried.

Then one day, something unexpected happened. The kids were once again picking on Michelle when the youngest Mackewitz kid, a scrawny little thing of about seven, broke away from her circle and ran over to the swings. I couldn't quite hear the exchange, but the next thing I knew the crowd had dispersed, and the Mackewitz kid was on the swing, pumping so hard that her dirty little skirt billowed about her like a balloon.

"He-he-he-he-he! He-he-he-he-he!" Michelle chortled. "You go fast! You go fast! Now my turn, MY TURN!" The girl jumped off the swing and Michelle got on. "Push me! PUSH!" It was an odd sight, the little kid pushing the full-bodied Michelle. But neither of them seemed to mind. They had each found a friend.

Why had the kids decided to leave Michelle alone? What could little Mackewitz have said that would have made that much difference? Maybe they were afraid her older siblings would rush to her defense and throttle them all, or maybe, like all bullies, they were simply unwilling to stand up to a challenge.

This compassion was from such an unexpected source, I didn't know what to make of it. What was it about Michelle that had brought out the Mackewitzes' warm and fuzzy side? I didn't know. But like Good Samaritans, they reached out to Michelle when this little Pharisee looked the other way. From that day on, as the Mackewitz pack made their way toward the school, you could always hear Michelle deep in their ranks. "He-he-he-he-he!"

—H.S.

Seventeen

Someone Watching Over Me

Through many dangers, toils, and snares
I have already come.
'Tis grace has brought me safe thus far,
And grace will lead me home.

"AMAZING GRACE" BY JOHN NEWTON

My visitor sat primly on the edge of my living room sofa, her teacup poised just below her narrow-set mouth. She was a seasoned career missionary. I was a rookie, and a short-termer at that. And so, when my friend Yashu was treed by the school's barking guard dogs after leaving my home after dinner one evening, Miss Julie decided it was time for us to talk.

"Really, Heidi, the problem is not the dogs," Miss Julie sniffed. "The problem is that *those people* should not be on school property after dark."

I wasn't sure I had heard her correctly. "Those people?"

"You know, the Africans."

"But they're my friends!"

Miss Julie sighed and set her teacup on the table. "We aren't supposed to befriend these people, Heidi. We're supposed to convert them. Otherwise they'll see that we're just like they are, and they won't want to become Christians."

I didn't know what to say. Every fiber of my being rebelled at the thought of relinquishing my church friends, who had made my first weeks in Senegal much less lonely. But the conversation had rattled me so, I was unable to form a proper response. Taking my silence for assent, Miss Julie bid me goodbye.

That Saturday evening after music practice, the sound of laughter and animated conversation followed me as I walked out of the church and made my way to the car by the light of the Senegalese moon. It had been a pleasant evening, and as I reached into my handbag to retrieve my car keys, a smile played on my lips. For the first time since I had arrived in Dakar, I was beginning to feel as though I fit in.

Playing keyboards for *La Lumieres* had provided me not only with an opportunity to serve, but with a wonderful source of friendships as well. Although I had not said as much to Miss Julie, I knew in my heart her approach to the Africans was wrong. *It's good that I've found friends so soon,* I told myself as I unlocked the driver's side of my VW Bug and slid inside, careful to lock the door behind me. We were not encouraged to travel alone at night; the dangers were not so much spoken as understood.

Inside the church, I could hear someone start up another chorus. Momentarily I debated going back inside, but decided that someone back at the mission house would be worrying about me. I leaned forward to put my key in the ignition.

Just then, a hand on my shoulder pulled me back.

Panicked, I froze, then glanced in the rearview mirror and

saw a strange man in my backseat. He scowled at me and ordered me in French to take him home. Now thoroughly terrified, I reached up a hand to unlock my door and get out, but he shoved me roughly again by the shoulder and signaled me to start the car. Afraid to do what he said, I sat still and waited, my head buzzing with stories of women who had disappeared without a trace.

Moments passed as we sat there. I prayed that someone ... *anyone* ... would walk by. At long last one of the men from the music group, Gondar, walked out the front door of the church and ambled toward the car. What a relief!

Gondar paused beside my car, but ignored me completely. Instead he ambled over to the passenger's side and spoke to the man behind me as if I wasn't there. I couldn't understand all that they said, but it seemed as though Gondar was inviting the man to his home for dinner. The man shook his head. Gondar then urged the man (a little more eagerly, I thought) to let me go on my way.

The man would not budge. "This woman will take me home, and then we'll see..." The menacing undertone was unmistakable.

My friend thought so, too. With a single motion Gondar reached through the open window, unlocked the car door, opened it, and dragged the stranger out by his arm. Then, casually leaning down to speak to me, he smiled and spoke to me the only English words I ever heard him speak. "Have a good evening." Both men then proceeded up the sidewalk toward Gondar's house. Dinner was waiting.

With shaking hands, I rolled up the window in the backseat, locked the door, and started the car. I did not know how the man had found his way into my backseat, nor how Gondar had known to rescue me. But one thing I did know for sure: I was never so thankful for my African friends as I was that very moment.

—H.S.

Eighteen

Ten Ways You Can Encourage Missionaries

1. *Stay in touch.* E-mail and letters help keep these special families from feeling isolated. Include church news, news clippings, comic strips–anything to give them a bit of home away from home.
2. *Don't expect too much.* Your family may not be able to respond to your letters as quickly or as frequently as you would like. They may feel discouraged or homesick, or as if they haven't much good news to report. Ask them how you can pray for them–and then do it.
3. *Remember birthdays and holidays.* A cheerful card signed by their "prayer team" or a small care package can really be an encouragement. The year she was in Africa, a group of friends sent Heidi a birthday card with a note saying that they would call at 2:00 on the afternoon of her birthday. She sat by that phone all day!
4. *Send care packages.* Some things that we take for granted— good Christian fiction or other popular books and magazines, chocolate chips, breakfast cereal, spaghetti, or pretty note cards—may not be readily available (or may be prohibitively expensive) where your missionaries live. Be sure to check with the sending agency or post office about the

best way to get packages to "your" family. (If you want an easy way to send a bag of chocolate chips or other small package, check out www.cravinghome.com.)

5. *Make videotapes.* Find out what shows your missionary friends enjoy—perhaps they followed a certain football team or weekly program—and record a whole tape's worth for them. Even the commercials! (Check to be sure they have a video player.)

6. *Keep your promises.* If you pledge support to them, make that a high priority in your budget. Whether it is a monthly check or a promise to pray, follow through.

7. *Don't put them on a pedestal.* Missionaries are just like you—they get discouraged, they get mad when their favorite sports team loses, and they love Snickers bars. You don't always have to talk about God or spiritual-sounding subjects when you're with them.

8. *Help them when they are home, too.* One church keeps a small apartment as a "home away from home" for their missionaries on furlough, to give them a bit of much-needed privacy. You may be able to help by storing some of their furniture or inviting them on a family picnic.

9. *Don't unload "junk."* Clothes that are worn or stained, broken appliances, and used tea bags belong in the trash, not in the missionary donation box. These families deserve the best we can give!

10. *Go the extra mile.* Missionaries sometimes incur unexpected expenses—someone gets sick or a generator breaks down. Find out where the needs are, and do what you can to help. Maybe your church youth group can sponsor a bake sale to raise the money they need!

Nineteen

My Polish Beauties

How, then, can they call on the one they have not believed in?
And how can they believe in the one whom they have not heard?
And how can they hear without someone preaching to them?
And how can they preach unless they are sent? As it is written,
"How beautiful are the feet of those who bring good news!"

ROMANS 10:14-15

I huddled at the back of the bus, praying that no one would try to find me. I was weary to the core of my being, and after five weeks on the road, I seriously doubted that I could lead this motley crew for one more day.

There were twenty-six of us on that Polish-American summer outreach team, not counting our Hungarian bus driver (who could communicate with us only in German, a language I had not spoken since high school). To make things even more interesting, thirteen members of the team were charismatics; the rest of us were predominantly Quakers or Baptists.

Only two of us spoke both Polish and English fluently— our translator, Roland, and our chaplain, a middle-aged American missionary who had helped to organize the itinerary.

I suspected that a few of the other Polish guys understood more than they let on, but it was a selective kind of thing. If they didn't like what was being said, they scowled and retorted, *"Nie rozumiem!"* ("I don't understand.") After this happened a few times, I uncovered the real problem: the Polish men considered it highly irregular for me, a woman, to be leading the group.

Not wanting to cause unnecessary controversy, and recognizing that from our host culture's perspective both our chaplain and our translator were better equipped to lead the team, I kept a low profile at first. But before the tour was over, our chaplain was summoned back to the United States by a family emergency and our translator returned home with his pregnant wife.

And so here I was, hiding in the back of the bus, only one sharp exchange away from total mutiny. In recounting my experiences later, I would tell people that I had been tested by fire that summer. Although now I can see that I was strengthened by the experience, at that time I could barely see through the smoke.

"There you are!" Grazyna's voice broke into my reverie behind the rack of metal music stands. "I wonder what happen to you."

Grazyna was about the last person I wanted to see at that moment. The tall brunette had all the fire of a redhead.

"What do you need, Grazyna?"

She looked at me thoughtfully, and I held my breath. "Are you OK?"

"Just a little tired."

"I pray for you," she declared.

Oh, help.

Firmly planting both hands on top of my head, she began to pray, first silently, then in a melodious prayer language, then finally in her broken English. "God, Heidi is your choice for us. She is our leader. Make her strong. Make her spirit strong. Help us now. Amen."

I had to admit her prayer made me feel better. "Thanks, Grazyna."

She winked at me. "No problem. Now come. We sing." And with that she stood and bellowed the first notes of a praise chorus, clapping and pointing until everyone had joined in praising our God.

The Polish women were a real godsend, I later reflected. None of them had much money, and most had no makeup or stockings or any of the other "performance essentials" so important to the American women. But the Polish sisters radiated a peaceful vitality that artificial beauty aids could not improve upon. More than once as we raided our own stash of stockings and mascara so the Polish women would not have to go without, I wished that just one of those women would return the favor by doling out a little of the effortless grace each of them wore like a crown.

I couldn't sleep. That afternoon we had received word that four of our Polish team members did not yet have the visas they needed to travel into Germany with the rest of the team. After a prolonged discussion, we had decided that I would travel with one of the Polish guys to the German embassy at Warsaw, and try to get the precious visas. If not, we would lose four musicians, including Grazyna and the one remaining Polish guy who spoke decent English.

I turned over and looked at my travel clock. Three in the morning. I planted my face in my pillow and sighed with the resignation of the doomed.

Just then I heard the soft rustle of cotton-clad feet and felt someone gently brush the top of my head. "Shhh..." I looked up and saw one of the Polish women sitting beside my cot. Ewa murmured something in Polish and smiled, then stroked a stray lock of hair from my cheek and began humming softly, like a mother to a restless infant. "Shhh..." I don't know how long I lay there, listening to her murmur and hum. I did not understand what she was saying, but as she prayed, the fearful burden that had gripped my chest released its hold. I slept dreamlessly, and awakened refreshed.

"How beautiful are the feet of those who bring good news," Scripture tells us. That summer I learned that for every well-shod soldier of Christ, there are a host of unseen hands, equally beautiful, polishing and lacing and tying those double knots. Though they are not drawn to the spotlight like so many moths, these servant warriors, silent and strong, are among the most beautiful creatures in God's great design.

—*H.S.*

Part Three

*G*od's Hands, at Home and
Around *the* World

y first experience on the mission field occurred when I was fifteen years old. My family went on a Caribbean cruise together. Our ship had been unable to dock at one of our destinations due to political unrest, and we were routed to Port-au-Prince, Haiti. Immediately upon docking, my sisters and I decided that we didn't want to go ashore. But our father insisted. It would be a valuable experience for us, he said.

As we walked along the dirt streets of Port-au-Prince that day, I experienced things I had previously only heard about when missionaries spoke at our church. In Port-au-Prince, dirty little children played in streets that smelled of urine and human waste. Young mothers and fathers with hollow eyes stood in the doorways of old, crumbling, one-room stucco houses. Elderly grandmothers and grandfathers, worn down by their impoverished existence, stared vacantly at us. Even the dogs and cats along the streets seemed to sense that this was a terrible place to live.

Since it was the customary thing to do, we decided to buy some souvenirs. Before we had disembarked from the cruise ship, we were advised by the crew to bargain with the merchants for any items that we wanted to buy rather than accept the stated price. The local merchants displayed wooden items such as little tables, maracas, and toys. There were also straw dolls and handbags, as well as handmade lace tablecloths and bedspreads.

My dad walked over to one merchant to check the price on an item that I wanted; he was told that it was $15. He offered the man $5 instead, and so the bargaining began. While Dad dickered with the merchant, I began to look around at the sights. The sadness of this poverty-stricken island got to me, and I started to cry. "Give him the $15, Dad," I begged my father. "Give him more than the $15. I'll pay the difference from my own money, if I need to. But I can't stand not giving these people money when they need it so badly!"

Even though I had ruined my dad's efforts at bargaining, my days of compassion and empathy toward those in need had begun. So far, I've taken eight missions trips overseas, and have worked with a couple of child-sponsorship organizations in my attempt to be a "missions-minded" Christian.

After reading this section, I hope that you, too, will be motivated to become God's hands. Whether you reach beyond your comfort zone to help others through prayer and friendship, with financial contributions, or by volunteering your time and skills for a special project or for full-time missionary service— either here or overseas—I hope you will feel the need to serve others, thus fulfilling the last command Jesus gave to us, his disciples:

> "All authority in heaven and on earth has been given to me. Therefore go and make disciples of all nations, baptizing them in the name of the Father and of the Son and of the Holy Spirit, and teaching them to obey everything I have commanded you. And surely I am with you always, to the very end of the age."
>
> MATTHEW 28:18-20

If you'd like to get involved, but don't know how, keep reading!

—*K.B.*

Twenty

Providing Bibles
Where There Are None

How beautiful on the mountains
  are the feet of those who bring good news,
who proclaim peace,
  who bring good tidings,
  who proclaim salvation,
who say to Zion,
    "Your God reigns!"

ISAIAH 52:7

4HIM members Marty Magehee, Mark Harris, Andy Chrisman, and Kirk Sullivan have been blessed with tremendous success. Seven albums—one of them gold—twenty number-one songs, six Dove Awards, and a Grammy Award nomination make 4HIM one of the most celebrated groups in contemporary Christian music. Following is an interview between Kim Boyce and Andy Chrisman about the work and needs of the American Bible Society, which the group has taken on as a cause.

KB: 4HIM has been working with the American Bible Society (ABS) since 1994. What made you decide to become spokesmen for this organization?

AC: ABS has one goal: to put the Word of God into the hands of everyone on the face of the earth. When we found out what the American Bible Society is all about, we realized that their heart matched ours. It's really an amazing thing they're doing. [Besides distributing Bibles,] they're also working to translate the Bible into every language in the world. It's a pretty daunting task they've got in front of them, but they're doing it.

KB: How have you partnered with ABS?

AC: Since ABS survives on contributions, we help raise money for them in our concerts. We've also actually taken Bibles overseas. We took four thousand Bibles to Russia. We thought it would take all day to hand out four thousand Bibles on the street corner, but they were gone in three minutes!

KB: Can you remember any person in particular who was affected by getting a Bible?

AC: I can think of a couple. The first was [a patient] in a children's hospital outside of Moscow. It's a hospital for kids who are missing limbs due to malnutrition or whatever. There were about four hundred children [in residence].

When we got there, we went into a room that housed about ten girls, and the interpreter told them about us. One of the girls immediately picked up a Russian children's Bible and showed it to us. It was a Bible that had been paid for out of donations we had raised. It blew my mind! That one Bible was shared by the ten girls in that hospital room. And that's how they got acquainted with Christ.

The president of ABS also told a story from China. A man who had run an underground church for about thirty years was captured by the government and put in prison for fifteen years. As he was released from prison, ABS workers were there and handed him a Bible in his Chinese dialect. Through an interpreter he told the workers that throughout his years of pastoring and imprisonment, he had never had a Bible. All he had had were some verses that a missionary had written on a few pieces of paper. There he was, seventy-something years old, walking out of a prison cell, and someone finally gave him his first Bible.

I wonder how many others there are like him—serving God, yet never having seen his Word. We take the Bible for granted. I'm looking at my bookshelf right now and I see at least eight Bibles; different translations, student Bibles, books that explain the Bible. We are so blessed.

KB: Andy, how do people get involved with ABS?

AC: The biggest need is for people to give money. The ABS is really one of those huge unsung organizations. My mom has been giving to the ABS for forty-something years, and up until five years ago, she was their typical donor, over fifty. They're trying to get their message out to the teen population. So they've had a push in the last few years to try to reach the younger generation with their message.

People need to understand that they don't have to give a lot.

Even if they give a quarter or a dollar, they're helping someone. ABS has different programs. They're actually involved in literacy programs, helping children learn to read in countries where education is not readily available. ABS helps children learn to read by giving them copies of a very easy-to-read children's Bible. Every dollar that you give to the American Bible Society immediately goes to helping someone in need. It doesn't funnel through a bunch of hands. If you give money, it goes for one thing—providing Bibles.

*For more information about
the American Bible Society, contact:*

ABS Interactive
1865 Broadway
New York, NY 10023
www.americanbible.org

Twenty-One

Streetwise in Brazil

It's not what you'd do with a million,
If riches should e'er be your lot,
But what are you doing at present
With the dollar and quarter you've got?

AUTHOR UNKNOWN

Since the 1950s, Compassion International has been one of the world's leading child-sponsorship organizations. With programs in twenty-two countries, Compassion International continues to meet the needs of impoverished children by providing food, clothing, education, and medical assistance as well as sound Bible teaching.

It was a balmy, tropical evening in Forteleza, Brazil. The male missionaries and members of our missions team encircled the female team members as we walked into the heart of an area of the city known for its thousands of street kids. The intense level of poverty in this densely populated city is such that parents find themselves unable to provide food for their children. In a misguided attempt at saving them, they force their children out of the home at a very early age.

Street children usually become the targets of drug dealers looking for runners to deliver their illegal substances. Many of the children, attempting to escape the horrors of their young lives, become junkies themselves. Still others become the victims of sexual abuse. For the price of a few pesos, something of infinite value is lost—the innocence, freedom, and happiness of childhood.

As we approached the area where thousands of street kids gathered, we saw a brother and sister sitting together on a blanket on the sidewalk. They looked up with sad eyes, asking passersby for money. The brother looked about five years old and his sister was probably three or so. Were these two children living alone on the streets?

I asked a missionary if the parents had positioned them here in order to beg for food or money. "No, Kim, those two are alone."

We soon approached a park crawling with street kids. Within seconds, we were being asked for money and food. The missionaries began speaking with the kids in Portuguese. "We don't have any food or money with us," they explained. But if the kids would follow us to a special mission center a couple of blocks away, they would receive a meal, a place to stay, and possibly even help in getting off the streets.

Most of the kids laughed and ran away. Three of them, however—two young boys and a girl—said they would go with us.

Several unbelievable things happened on our short walk. First, one of the boys pick-pocketed the watch of a female team member. Our missionary leader saw the incident and forced him to return the watch.

Within seconds, both boys ran out into the middle of traffic and jumped onto the back bumper of a city bus. They proceeded to squat down, grab hold of the large rubber bumper of the bus and swing themselves underneath the rear of the bus with their arms and legs wrapped around the bumper. Their backs were just inches above the pavement that was racing beneath them! Our team members watched in shock as these boys disappeared from sight as the bus rushed down the street.

Only the girl, Nubia, was left to go with us to the mission center. When we arrived, Nubia was given a hot bowl of rice and beans. This was most likely the only hot meal she had had in weeks. She ate the food voraciously. Then as she finished her meal, she looked up and asked, "Now who do I have to sleep with?"

Nubia's eyes grew wide as the missionaries explained to her that she would not have to sleep with anyone or pay them for her meal in any other way. When she was told that she could spend the night at the mission center in a comfortable bed and she could take a shower and put on clean clothes, she was speechless. She had never known such kindness.

Nubia had just begun an incredible journey. If she would agree to report to the center nightly and obey the center's rules for ninety days, she would be trained in a vocational skill that would enable her to work, rather than live her life on the streets. She would then be able to live and work with a specially chosen family in a rural area of Brazil. This Christian family would become Nubia's family. They would take her into their home and love and train her along with their own children. What an incredible change for Nubia!

—K.B.

For more information about
Compassion International, contact:

Compassion International
Colorado Springs, CO 80997 U.S.A.
(719) 594-9900
www.compassioninternational.com

Twenty-Two

How Can You Fight World Hunger?

Most of us have no idea what it is like to be truly hungry, and to not know where our next meal is coming from. However, there are millions of people all over the world who are not so lucky. How can you help?

1. Consider sponsoring a child through a program such as Compassion International. For just dollars each month, you can make a difference in the life of one child. You may sponsor a child individually or as part of a group–a Sunday school class or youth group, for example.

2. Hunger hits closer to home than you might think. Your own town probably has soup kitchens that could use donations of food or time. If you do not know of one, check in the phone books for service organizations such as Food Gatherers, or contact your local health and human services department.

3. Participate in the "30 Hour Famine" program sponsored by World Vision to help feed hungry families all over the world. Contact www.30hourfamine.org or 1-800-7FAMINE for more information.

4. Feeding the hungry can be as simple as surfing the Net. Log on to www.hungersite.com, and with a simple click of your mouse, corporate sponsors donate a half cup of food to hungry people all over the world. That's it! No purchase is necessary. Of course, if you *do* like to shop online, check out www.thehungersite.greatergood.com. Fifteen percent of each purchase goes to the United Nations World Food Program.

Twenty-Three

"The Way to My Heart Is Through My Kids"

If Jesus Christ be God and died for me,
then no sacrifice can be too great for me to make for him.

C.T. STUDD

Bob Carlisle deserves many accolades for his long career in contemporary Christian music, but he will always be remembered for a special love song—"Butterfly Kisses." As Kim talked with Bob about his involvement with Food For The Hungry, she was touched to discover the reason for his involvement: he did it for his own family.

KB: Bob, I understand that Food For The Hungry (FH) is your first venture into actually promoting a charitable organization.

BC: Yeah, it is. [FH] approached me as an artist and asked if I would align myself with them. I told them "No" because I didn't feel great about those types of relationships. I won't do anything unless my heart is in it. I can tend to be an old, jaded, cynical guy. I don't like seeing children on television with flies in their eyes being held by someone who claims that I care more about the price of a cheeseburger than the life of that child.... There's only one way to my heart and that's through *my* kids. That's the direct route to me.

KB: What changed your mind?

BC: I genuinely liked Rory Starkes, executive director at Food For The Hungry. He took my family and me down to the Dominican Republic with no obligation to represent them, just to go see what they're doing. I thought it would be a wonderful opportunity for my kids. Both my children—my daughter especially—have wonderful, warm, compassionate hearts for people who are less fortunate than we are. So we went to the Dominican Republic, and to make a long story short, we went out into the villages and saw the devastation.

I went, expecting that it was somehow my obligation to fall in love with the mission, and I was a bit cynical about that. But I went down and found myself falling in love with the *missionaries*. I had never before seen it that way. I saw my daughter interacting with them, and was impressed to the extent that she wanted to stay and help these people who were in the trenches, not making any money, volunteering their time.

As I walked down the mud-gutted streets, we saw little children come out and run around the FH volunteers. There were tears of joy and laughter. The volunteers were a part of this community. They weren't there because it was of benefit to them in any way other than that they were just serving God. And I felt guilty because I had been so crusty and jaded. It was amazing. I fell in love with what they were doing. I fell in love with their hearts.

KB: I've heard a lot of stories from people who have been touched by a particular child or incident and decided to work with an organization as a result, but I haven't been told before that someone was moved by the hearts of the missionaries involved. That's great!

After my interview with Bob Carlisle, I had the opportunity to attend a weekend retreat with several Food For The Hungry staff members. During our time together, I became aware of these staff members' unwavering dedication to their ministry. Later I interviewed the executive vice president of Food For The Hungry, Rory Starkes, to find out more about the organization.

KB: You've been involved in missions work for a long time.

RS: Yes, in the past fifteen years, I have worked in more than twenty third-world countries. I have looked into the tear-filled eyes of a mother who had lost a child to hunger. I've celebrated with tribal men who were praising God for recent rains that followed a long drought. I have witnessed the joy and suffering of families struggling to survive in the harsh context of a developing country.

KB: On your last trip to Ethiopia, you had a unique experience.

RS: Yes, the evening before we were to drive to the village of Gondar, I was reflecting on how easy it is to lose touch with the humanity of the poor. I had become so used to seeing poverty that I needed the Lord to touch my heart again. My prayer was simple: *"Lord, let me see Jesus in the eyes of the poor."*

We left early the next morning to visit Gondar, which had been severely affected by the recent drought in Ethiopia. [The villagers] had no food. Crops had failed. Their only source of "food" was weeds they boiled in saltwater for their children to eat!

KB: Did you see any of these children?

RS: Yes, a group of them came forward out of the crowd, and they were, indeed, malnourished. As I scanned the group of children, one of them stepped toward me. She was probably nine or ten years old. Her little body was shivering from the cold. She had no energy reserves to warm her weakened body. Her arms and legs, even her head was shaking. As she stood there, looking at me, I felt as if I was looking into the eyes of Jesus. My eyes were fixed on hers and hers on mine.

It was one of the most profound moments of my life. I had prayed that Jesus would reveal himself to me, but I didn't expect it to be through a little girl. Yet there he was, looking up at me, "one of the least of these."

KB: What did you do?

RS: Regrettably, nothing. Then I noticed one of my colleagues had taken off his shirt. He knelt down in front of the little girl and pulled his shirt over her head. Then he began to rub her shivering arms. Within five minutes or so, she stopped shivering. She was warm again!

As I watched my colleague warm the shivering little girl, I realized: they die one at a time ... they can be helped one at a time. You and I can't help every child, but we can make a difference in the life of one. The next time God prompts you to help someone, do it! Don't analyze it. Don't question it. Just do it! And most importantly, do it as unto the Lord.

—*K.B.*

For more information on
Food For The Hungry, contact:

Food For The Hungry
7729 East Greenway Road
Scottsdale, AZ 85260
www.fh.org

Twenty-Four

Heaven's Outpost

I care not if God is on my side. My constant hope and prayer is that I may be found on God's side.

ABRAHAM LINCOLN

Gary and I met Pastor Phil Greenaway at a missions banquet a year before this story opens. He invited us to sing at his church if we were ever in New York. When we decided to take him up on his offer, we discovered that the Church in the Village was unlike any church we had ever visited. This ministry touched our hearts profoundly and continues to encourage us today in reaching out to those who are "different."

The taxi driver dropped us off on the corner. Gary and I were supposed to be singing at a place called the Church in the Village in New York City that evening, but as we looked around, we didn't see a church anywhere. We did, however, hear music coming through the open windows of a nearby building. As we walked toward the sound, we saw the nondescript sign on the side of the building. We were in the right place after all.

We entered the building and listened to the multi-racial praise band for a moment before being led downstairs into the basement to meet with Pastor Greenaway and discuss the Friday evening worship service. I remembered what the pastor had told me the previous year at that missions banquet: "This is not your ordinary church, but I know our people would enjoy your ministry."

In order to afford the exorbitant rent in that part of the city, the Church in the Village shares an auditorium with two other churches. In addition, Pastor Greenaway travels extensively throughout the year raising money to support the ministry. Many of the members of his congregation can barely make ends meet, and could never fully support this much-needed work on their own. The Church in the Village is truly a "home missions" work.

We were anxious to participate in this culturally diverse, very up-tempo worship experience, although as we went upstairs and waited to sing, I began to worry that our concert would be too "homogenized" for this congregation. But my fears were put to rest as we were greeted with a warm reception and enthusiastic participation throughout the concert. One woman accepted the Lord as we prayed together at the evening's end.

What Gary and I experienced that night in the Church in the Village could be described as a "Spirit-led bond." We hadn't expected to be drawn to this group of people from completely different backgrounds and cultures, but as we talked with some of the people there, we felt a unique connection with them. One handsome young man whom Gary talked with at length had particularly captured our interest because his face was cut and bruised. Although we didn't ask him about his wounds,

Pastor Greenaway told us later that this young man was homeless. Some other homeless men had beaten him just a few days before.

The East Village is home to many young runaways and homeless youth who have come to this part of New York City for the thrills. In fact, there were many homeless people at our concert that night. There were also alcoholics and drug addicts in various stages of recovery, abuse victims, and scores of broken families. Even while we were singing, Pastor Greenaway had had to leave to go downstairs and settle a domestic dispute that was about to come to blows.

This pastor has answered God's call to serve in a desperately needed place of ministry. His church is an outpost of heaven on the shores of hell. In a neighborhood riddled with New Age, witchcraft, and bondage shops, Pastor Greenaway is reaching out to those who are hurting in ways that most of us in middle class America could never begin to relate to or understand.

As we drove to our hotel that evening, I thought about the people we had just met. Many of them would find their dinner in a fast-food restaurant dumpster and sleep on a park bench—in the middle of one of the wealthiest cities in the world. Thank God for Pastor Greenaway and the untold hundreds and thousands of pastors, missionaries, and lay workers who are called to eternally rewarding work. In spite of the financial pressures, long hours, and the sorrow of watching people self-destruct, these workers continue to fight the good fight. Keep up the good work. Your reward will be great!

—*K. B.*

Twenty-Five

Healing Hands

I don't want you to give me your surplus.
I want you to give with personal deprivation.

MOTHER TERESA

Joyce Martin McCollough, Jonathan Martin, and Judy Martin Hess were raised in an eight hundred-square foot house without electricity in rural Arkansas. Their mother taught them to sing for daily entertainment. Soon their extraordinary harmonies were being heard all over the Midwest.

Their big break came in 1992, when they sang a cappella in a ladies' restroom for Gloria Gaither. The rest, as they say, is history. Several albums, awards, and thousands of concerts later, these siblings haven't forgotten where they came from, and now they're reaching out to others in need. Joyce was kind enough to share some of the details:

KB: The American Leprosy Mission (ALM) is just starting to work with Christian artists. Are you their first?

JM: We were one of the first. We may have been the first to take their message "on-the-road."

KB: I must admit that I'm probably like most of the people whom you share ALM with in concert. I didn't even realize there was still a leprosy problem in the world.

JM: I didn't either. There used to be a leper colony right here in the United States, just four hours from where I live. I didn't even know it.

KB: I was thinking about the movie *Ben Hur,* when Charleston Heston's character goes out to a leper colony to visit his mother and sister. It was heartbreaking to see these people who were completely outcast from society because of their disease.

JM: Yes. Leprosy affects the nervous system, and those with the disease eventually lose feeling in their limbs. Then they can break bones or actually knock limbs off and not even feel pain. And there's also the terrible appearance of disfigured skin that leprosy produces.

KB: It's astounding to me that there are still about 150 cases of leprosy reported in the United States every year, and *700,000 cases worldwide.* But according to ALM's information, it only takes $200 worth of medicine to completely cure a case of leprosy.

JM: That's what compelled us to be a part of ALM. To think that for a relatively small amount of money, we can *cure* someone of this horrible disease.

KB: According to ALM, your family has already raised enough support to cure six hundred leprosy cases.

JM: Yes, and our goal for this tour is a thousand cured cases. We're not yet halfway through the tour, so we're now hoping we can do more than the original goal of one thousand. Working with ALM has really made a difference in our lives. Now after each concert, we go back to the bus and start figuring up how many cases of leprosy we've been able to raise the money to cure!

—K.B.

Would you like to help?
Contact the American Leprosy Mission at:

One ALM Way
Greenville, SC 29601
www.leprosy.org

Twenty-Six

A Message of Love
for a New Generation

Happiness is about having someone to love you, in a way—if the someone is really Someone.... C.S. Lewis said that we bear, all our lives, an "inconsolable longing," an innate awareness of our incompleteness that is, ultimately, only resolved when we are present with the Lord.

STACY AND PAULA RINEHART

Sexual Health and Relationship Education (SHARE) is an organization based in Seattle, Washington, that educates single men and women on the value of chastity. In 1998, SHARE presented its message of abstinence before marriage to over twenty-six thousand students and helped more than thirty communities form successful abstinence programs. SHARE also trains speakers on communicating the message of abstinence. Kim had the privilege of meeting SHARE's executive director, Carrie Abbot, and her family when she sang at the LifeChoices annual fund-raising banquet in Seattle.

KB: Tell me how the SHARE program got started.

CA: [SHARE] was started in 1987, by a group of people who worked with our crisis pregnancy center, LifeChoices. They wanted a pregnancy prevention program, so they put together the abstinence program that we have today. They started the program by bringing speakers into churches to address students, and then SHARE started going into public schools to encourage sexual abstinence. We now have more than fifty speakers, and eighty percent of the students we reach are in public schools. We've also started thirteen other programs in Washington, outside the Seattle area, and another twenty programs around the country. In order to help others start similar programs in their cities, we offer training in the use of our curriculum. I've also written a manual [explaining] how to start a program like this in any community.

KB: What qualities matter most if you're dealing with teens on this issue?

CA: When you're dealing with teens and relationship building, you have to be available. You'll have greater impact in teens' lives if you're someone from their area rather than a guest speaker who flies in to speak one time. Volunteers have an even greater impact on teens. When students find out that our speakers don't get paid, they don't understand why they would take time out of their schedule or use their day off to help them. [Our volunteers] send a valuable message to the students: "You are worth my time. You're valuable." That's one of the reasons our program works so well.

KB: When did you get involved with SHARE?

CA: In 1989, I came in as a speaker, and after three or four years I ended up as the director. I was pregnant with my second child when I started. We have five children now, so I've had four of them since I started going into schools and connecting with kids.

KB: Why would you give your time when you have five children of your own?

CA: When I was seventeen I started working with the youth in my own church. I have always worked with this age group. Some people are afraid of teens; I'm not. I love connecting with them. I know it's a critical time in their lives in junior high and high school, when they're making life-changing decisions. And when mistakes are made in the area of sexual purity, it causes a great deal of pain and heartache. Some people get involved in drugs, some in alcohol, but generally [it's] in the areas of dating, relationships, and sex that they mess up for the long term.

KB: In addition to your ministry to teens, you are also a wife and mother of five children, whom you homeschool. How does that work? How do you take care of five kids—let alone homeschool them—and still have time to serve with SHARE?

CA: My theme is, "My life is not my own." Along with teaching my own children, I need to share the gift that God gave me as a speaker; that's my job while I'm here. I want my children to grow up in a healthy generation. I may sacrifice a lot of time, but I don't sacrifice my children. When you are called by God, he gives you grace to do what he's called you to. Your family doesn't have to suffer—and if they do suffer, something's wrong. So my husband's job is to keep me in balance!

KB: Do you take your children with you when you speak?

CA: Except for my oldest, my children have not heard me speak because they're too young to hear the SHARE message. My oldest son, who is thirteen, just sat in my class for the first time a month ago. I was able to teach him, along with a hundred other kids in the youth group, God's plan for his sexuality. Later he said how wonderful it is for him to have a mom who understands these things.

—*K.B.*

For more information about SHARE, contact:

SHARE
15935 NE 8th St., Suite B-200
Bellevue, WA 98008-3918
(877) 44SHARE
www.share-program.com

Twenty-Seven

Bringing God's Mercy
to Girls in Trouble

Out of the depths I cry to you, O Lord;
O Lord, hear my voice.
Let your ears be attentive
to my cry for mercy.
If you, O Lord, kept a record of sins,
O Lord, who could stand?
But with you there is forgiveness;
therefore you are feared.
I wait for the Lord, my soul waits,
and in his word I put my hope.

PSALM 130:1-5

*S*ince their debut in 1992, Point of Grace has had twenty-one consecutive number-one radio singles. Since they started singing together in college, Shelley Breen, Denise Jones, Heather Payne, and Terry Jones have recorded four gold and one platinum album and have numerous Dove and Grammy Awards. Their rise in contemporary Christian music has been meteoric, and yet those who know these four long-time friends personally say they haven't *changed a bit. I recently interviewed Heather about Mercy Ministries of America.*

KB: What made Point of Grace want to get involved with another ministry?

HP: Our manager had just adopted a baby through Mercy Ministries. We had no idea what the ministry was about until we heard about it through him. We saw the whole process and how much joy it brought into his life, and we began praying about our involvement.

We actually got together with Nancy Alcorn, president of Mercy Ministries. We visited and it was like, "Look no more." We knew that this was the ministry we wanted to be involved in. We even got to talk to the girls ... to see how God was working in their lives.

Some of the girls had been involved in gangs. Many [were] hard on the outside, but you could tell there was softness and tenderness on the inside. They had been through so much, and yet they had received the unconditional love and mercy of God. We wanted to be a part of that.

But you know, a lot of girls who were there were pastors' daughters who had gotten pregnant or had gotten involved in eating disorders. So it wasn't just girls who were involved in gangs, it was girls who were ... like me! It could have been me.

So we got involved. Nancy has traveled with us on the road, and has had opportunities to talk about this ministry. She's raised a lot of money being on the road with us, people giving every month. It really has been awesome, seeing how God has provided for them, sometimes at the very last minute. They aren't sponsored by the government in any way.

The stories of God's provision for the ministry are amazing. Once they got a big light bill and didn't know how they would pay it. All of a sudden they got a check in the mail for the exact amount of the light bill! Stories like that make you say, "OK, God's in this ministry."

I had lunch yesterday with a girl who graduated from Mercy Ministry who's on the road with us now, sharing her testimony. [Her participation] shows you not just what's going on during the program, but what's happening in [the girls'] lives afterward. They still have struggles.

The ministry teaches the girls how to cook and how to clean and how to live in the real world. Many of them, though, are dealing with so much that once they get out on their own, it all kind of overwhelms them. Some girls come back two or three times to the home.

KB: It sounds like even after working with Mercy Ministries for years, you're still excited about it.

HP: Even more than before, I think. We can see how God continues to bless the ministry. His hand continues to be on it. Of course, in any ministry, complacency sets in. The good thing is [that] Nancy has people in her life keeping her accountable and advising her. That's security for us. This ministry is grounded on the Word of God and in faith that God will provide. And he has. He has provided from the very beginning. Many times if we have a spiritual question, we'll go to Nancy. I'm honored to call her a friend.

KB: It's great to hear about Mercy Ministries from someone who is excited about it and knows firsthand stories of the girls and what they've been through.

HP: You know what's really neat? The graduations! Shelley and I went to one graduation in November to support one girl who didn't have any family. At the graduation ceremony they gave the girls a ring to signify their graduation from the program. Now I want to go to every graduation! It was the most amazing thing!

Each girl tells the story of what God has done in her life, and then someone on staff [talks about] the changes they've seen in the girls' lives. If the girls' parents are there, they can say something too. It's a joyful, laughter-through-tears kind of thing. At the end of the ceremony, the counselors who have worked with the girls commission them; they pray over them before they go back out into the world.

This graduation ceremony completes the process. It signifies that these girls have given their lives over to God and said, "OK, I'm going to make a difference in the world. I'm going to walk upright and with integrity." It's very cool. I tell you what, the more I go over there, the more I want to go over there.

One thing that Mercy Ministries emphasizes with the girls is that they—all of us—are complete in Christ. I need to be reminded of that too, sometimes. Our identity is in Christ and nothing else. That's where the joy comes from.

—*K.B.*

For more information about Mercy Ministries, contact:

Mercy Ministries of America
P.O. Box 111060
Nashville, TN 37222
(615) 831-6987

Twenty-Eight

Romanian Tears

The proper time to influence the character of a child is about a
hundred years before he is born.

WILLIAM RALPH INGE

In February of 1990, I was part of a five-member missions team
to Romania. The trip took place six weeks after the fall of com-
munism in the country, so it was in a state of political upheaval.
Among the worst affected were the children of Romania; thousands of parents, unable to care for their families because of the eco-
nomic collapse that followed the political turmoil, sent their children to government-run orphanages.

Just prior to our mission trip, a U.S. television news magazine
had exposed the deplorable conditions of these institutions. One person in the group had seen the program and was interested in
adopting a Romanian child, and so we were permitted to visit one
of the orphanages.

On the appointed afternoon, we arrived at the gates of the
orphanage. From the outside, the buildings looked run-down,
and there was no evidence that children lived there. We didn't

see any playground equipment on the compound, or children at play. We rang the bell; the woman in charge of the orphanage greeted us and our tour began.

Through an interpreter she told us about the children in the orphanage. Many were mentally impaired and could not be adopted because of their condition. Children less than three years of age could not be adopted without parental consent. The woman explained that under communist law, parents who were unable to care properly for children under the age of three could leave them at an orphanage, where they would be cared for by the government. However, any children left at the orphanage past their third birthday were immediately eligible for adoption.

We walked through room after room and ward after ward filled with infants and children under the age of three. Most of these children spent their days in a metal crib on a hard mattress, some without sheets or blankets, even on the coldest of winter days. The majority of the children looked perfectly normal, but they had the saddest eyes I have ever seen. A few were playful and responsive, but most sat or lay listlessly in their cribs. These children had no vibrancy, no life—no hope. The atmosphere was more like you'd expect in an old people's home, but this was a nursery! It broke my heart to see the sorrow in their little faces. They were already acquainted with heartbreak that would break the spirits of most adults. It was certainly no way for a child to live.

We were then taken into a play area where a group of about twenty two-year-olds were playing. The room was bare except for four child-size tables formed in a square and surrounded by chairs. At one point, the children ran to the table and quickly sat in their chairs and became very quiet. I assumed that it was time for a snack because of their enthusiasm and obedience when the teacher spoke to them. When they sat down and were quiet, a small tin cup was given to each child. The teacher then came around and poured water into each cup. A cup of water was their special treat!

There is no happy ending to this story. We left that day with sad hearts, and three days later we left Romania. I don't know what became of those children. I have prayed many times that their parents came back for them or that they were adopted by wonderful, caring families. If you have been moved by this story, please pray with me: "Lord, I can only do so much, but use me somehow, someway, however you see fit."

—*K.B.*

Jesus answered, "Everyone who drinks this water will be thirsty again, but whoever drinks the water I give him will never thirst. Indeed, the water I give him will become in him a spring of water welling up to eternal life."

JOHN 4:13-14

Twenty-Nine

A Chernobyl Victim

Hope is the power of being cheerful in circumstances which we know to be desperate.

G.K. CHESTERTON

My manager, Joe Battaglia, serves on the board of CitiHope International. When I told Joe I was working on this book, he suggested I talk with his friend, Paul Moore, the president and founder of this organization, about the incredible work it has been doing since 1985. CitiHope International has brought relief to needy individuals both in the United States and the former Soviet Union.

In fulfilling their mission, "Establishing a Christian society by promoting spiritual, mental, and physical health care worldwide," CitiHope provides medicine and medical supplies as well as food products and other relief items to those in need in Belarus, Ukraine, Russia, and five other New Independent State Republics; Romania; and Macedonia.

KB: I understand that CitiHope has been involved in giving aid to the victims of the Chernobyl disaster. How did you come to be involved in this ministry?

PM: On a trip to Germany and Russia, Dr. Michael Christensen, my son, Paul Jr., and I met the children of Chernobyl. We saw dying kids triaged in two principal hospitals in Minsk, Belarus.

KB: They were put there to die?

PM: Oh, absolutely. The hospitals had no Western medicine, or even knowledge of contemporary oncological protocols! Four years before, these kids had been exposed to the mushroom cloud that covered the northern Ukraine and radioactive-contaminated rain that came down for ten days. The cloud blew north and west over Belarus; the contaminants were a hundred times more intense in their density than those that fell at Hiroshima or Nagasaki. Because they ingested large amounts of contaminated food and breathed the air, tens of thousands of citizens have become sick, many of them with cancer.

We went into these darkened hospitals and saw doctors giving mothers placebos (sugar pills) for their children, so they could feel like they were doing something. Mother after mother would place little Tatiana, Tonya, Victor, or Pavel in my arms and fall to her knees, begging me to take the baby to America where it might survive.

As a result of that experience, Paul Jr. and I dedicated ourselves to getting as much help as possible—medically, nutritionally, economically, and spiritually—to the people of the former

Soviet Union. And that was the beginning of CitiHope.

KB: The people must appreciate what you're doing in these countries.

PM: These people are so hospitable. They are the most kind, generous, open, intelligent, artistic people I've ever encountered. They had more fear of the U.S. during the Cold War than we did of them. Now we were able to bring reconciliation. We brought the first Christmas celebration back to that part of the world. Because of what we did for people in the name of Christ, we were given favor and opportunities. The rapid evangelization that followed, the rebirth of spiritual life, has been unequaled. The simplicity of the gospel is so powerful and persuasive.

I love what we're doing. We are now in Kyrgyzstan, Azerbaijan, Armenia, the Ukraine. The U.S. Department of State is primarily funding our use of Soviet aircraft. We fly the aircraft into Holland and load them up with medical supplies and equipment, and then once a month we fly into one of our countries. We've delivered over $240 million worth of medicine. We have a new contract to deliver another ten airlifts over the next two years. We bring American volunteers ... doctors, economists, clergy, wonderful Christian laity come to serve.

KB: I understand that when he was seventeen, your son's life was touched through his work at CitiHope. Can you tell me about that?

PM: When Paul Jr. was seventeen, he met a fourteen-year-old girl named Natasha at the hospital. She was dying of Hodgkins lymphoma. In one day, these two found each other and fell in love. Not a physical relationship, though romantic, and one that was spiritually deep. He was able to lead her to Christ.

We came back two months later to bring medicine to the hospital. Natasha said, "I know where I'm going. I know I'm dying. But outside these doors are kids you can still save. I've told them that they can count on you." Though Natasha was once a vibrant, gorgeous, young ballerina, Chernobyl had reduced her to a seventy-pound cancer victim. As my son held her hand, she asked, "Could we dance?" She had not been out of bed in nine months.

Paul said to her, "You can't, you're too weak."

She replied, "Would you get up in the room and dance? And in my imagination, I will dance with you." And so, as uncomfortable as it was for him, Paul got up and danced to a Petra song on cassette. She lay in her bed and joined him in her mind. Then with tears streaming down her face, she took his hand and said, "I know that one day in heaven we will dance across the fields."

That was the last time Paul saw Natasha alive. One day he received a letter from a Swiss doctor who had happened by Natasha's hospital room. The doctor had a camera and had promised Natasha he would send Paul her picture with this note. It said, "Here's a picture. Today I stood up. I'm standing up for you. I'm standing up for Jesus. I'm standing up for all the kids outside my door. We are young, but we can change the world." Paul received this letter two weeks after we had heard she had died.

Paul has since taken probably a dozen teenagers with him to

Belarus where they have volunteered and gone to hospitals—unloading trucks, delivering supplies to hospitals, visiting children in the cancer wards. And they're the best! Many of these kids have never seen cancer up close like this, and so the teens often come back from the experience deeply affected by what they have seen—and more in tune with the needs of others at home.

—*K.B.*

For more information about
CitiHope International, contact:

CitiHope International
P.O. Box 38, Main Street
Andes, NY 13731
(914) 676-4400
CitiHopeCH@aol.com

Thirty

You Can't Out-Give God

Our desire is not that others might be relieved while you are hard pressed, but that there might be equality. At the present time your plenty will supply what they need, so that in turn their plenty will supply what you need. Then there will be equality.

2 CORINTHIANS 8:13-14

Christian humorist and singer Mark Lowry has gold albums and videos, Dove and Grammy Awards, and three GMA Grady Nutt Humor Awards. He's the author of five books, four of which are a series of children's books, and he's a long-time member of the Gaither Vocal Band.

When I met Mark fifteen years ago, he was traveling around the country in a car from church to church. I was working behind the scenes at a Christian TV station where Mark came as a guest on a show. A lot has happened in these last fifteen years.

Recently my family and I met Mark for dinner in Nashville. After many laughs and a great meal, we got down to the business at hand...

KB: Tell me your philosophy on giving.

ML: So I gotta get in *that* mode! OK. It's like the law of gravity—you know, you've heard people say all your life, "Don't break God's laws." Well, no one ever breaks God's laws—they break you [if you don't follow them]. Madeline Murray O'Hare or Billy Graham, it doesn't matter.

The law of gravity applies to everyone, believer or not. Christian or Jew. Buddhist or atheist. The law of gravity applies.

I also believe in the law of sowing and reaping; it works. I believe it works because you can't out-give God. It doesn't matter why it works. It just does. It has nothing to do with being spiritual and it has everything to do with being a good businessman. I believe in giving to [organizations] that feed children, take care of widows and orphans—because that's what Jesus said to do. He is [the One] I follow, so I think that makes sense. What concerns him should concern me.

It's impossible to out-give God. He's not going to let it happen. And I don't believe that [giving] all has to be done through the local church. There are tithes and there are offerings. You're the steward. I've heard preachers all my life preach on giving percent. Big deal, that's nothing. Jesus told the rich young ruler, "Sell it all and follow me." Jesus didn't destroy the law. He fulfilled it. And he raised the standard. In the Old Testament, you commit adultery, you've sinned. In the New Testament, you even think about it, you've sinned. In the Old Testament, God wanted percent; in the New Testament, Jesus said, "Sell it all and follow me."

KB: You give to an AIDS ministry.

ML: There's a lady in Fresno, California who has a ministry called "All About Care" for women and children infected with and affected by AIDS. Her husband died of AIDS back in 1985, and she didn't know anything about the disease. She now has a great ministry. She can take a dollar and turn it into three or four. She's a good steward.

Everybody just needs to know who and what they're giving to. It's that simple. You take tomato seeds and you throw them on the interstate, don't expect a harvest. You take the seed that God has given you, and you give it to some TV evangelist with an 800 number on the screen saying, "Give to God," and he's pointing in his [own] direction.... You need to check him out. He could be winning the world to Christ, feeding children, and clothing the naked. Or he could be building a mansion in Palm Springs. You need to know what the soil's like.

You need to do some investigating to make sure [the ministry] is doing what they say they're doing. And I checked out All About Care. I've been supporting it for quite a few years. I give to All About Care and someone's electricity stays on. Someone's going to get to have a Thanksgiving dinner because I was on this earth. It is amazing what can be done with so little.

So, [being] a good steward means, number one, that you give. Number two, you check out who you're giving to and you hold them responsible. Not to the point that if they don't have the piano on the right side of the church, you won't give to that church. Don't let your preferences get in the way of God making you a channel through whom his blessings can flow. But if they're worshiping Buddha, you've got a problem!

—K.B.

For more information on All About Care,
contact Cynthia Karraker at (559) 222-9471.

Thirty-One

Tips to Help You Give Wisely

How many times have you turned on the television or opened a magazine and found your heartstrings being pulled by some organization soliciting donations? The work they do sounds good—feeding hungry children, providing indigent communities with safe drinking water, bringing the gospel to thousands of people who have never heard of Jesus. But how much of your money is being spent on those projects? How much is allocated to administrative costs and marketing campaigns?

We want to help—and yet, it's not always easy to tell which organizations are really helping the people who need it most. Here are some ways that you can get the information you need to make wise choices about where your money goes.

- *Don't allow yourself to be emotionally blackmailed into giving.* Be wary of high-pressure phone appeals that stress emotion and sentimentality over facts and figures. Worthwhile charitable organizations will provide the information you need to help you make a wise decision.
- *Check an organization's credibility rating before giving.* The Better Business Bureau (www.bbb.org) prepares a quarterly

newsletter entitled "Give but Give Wisely" that rates over two hundred commonly asked-about charities. Crown Financial Ministries (formerly Christian Financial Concepts) (770-534-1000; www.cfcministry.org) has a free pamphlet called "Giving and Tithing" that will give you other good ideas for giving wisely. Your pastor or denominational head-quarters may also know of good sources of information.

- *Don't give to charitable organizations that refuse to give you written information about their finances and purpose.* Excuses such as "It's too expensive" or "We only send information to those who make a pledge" demonstrate a lack of good faith.
- *Ask God what he wants you to do.* Don't let yourself be pressured, flattered, or "guilted" into being an unwise steward of the resources God has entrusted to you. Take the time you need to give prayerful consideration to a request.

If you sense that God is putting a certain organization or specific need on your heart, give generously, for "God loves a cheerful giver" (2 Co 9:7). On the other hand, if you are having trouble deciding what God is asking of you, talk with someone whose character and spiritual maturity you trust. God doesn't expect you to single-handedly eradicate all the poverty in the world. However, as God's children we become a powerful testimony to the love and compassion of the Lord when we reach out in his name to those who need it most.

Part Four

A Circle of Love:
Lessons *in* Caring

The phone jangled me out of a sound sleep. Groggy, I groped for my glasses and peered at the clock. Six A.M. Unbelievable. There was only one person in the world it could be.

A few months before, I had met Donna at a young adult group at church. Donna struggled with depression and had just started taking medication to help her regulate her mood swings. But when she felt really down, she always called me to pray her through.

Irritated, I grabbed the phone. "Yes, Donna …"

Instead of Donna's voice, I heard another friend's voice on the line. "Heidi, I just took Donna to the hospital. She says she wants to kill herself, and this time I think she means it. Please pray."

I promised I would and hung up, trying to grasp what I had just heard. Donna, suicidal? Despite her mood swings and depression, the thought that she might consider suicide had never occurred to me.

A few days later, when she was up to receiving visitors, I visited Donna in the hospital. She looked a little tired, but she smiled when she saw me in the hallway. Her hair, which was usually pulled back in a ponytail with a scrunchy, hung loose around her shoulders. I had no idea what to say to her, so I just sat with her awhile, and then offered to pray with her. A few days later, Donna was well enough to be released.

Six months later, life knocked me flat. My best friend and her family moved over a thousand miles away, and a few weeks later my boyfriend and I broke up. Just when I thought it couldn't get any worse, my back went out. I could have handled any one of these three things without missing a beat, but the three events combined launched me into the mother of all pity parties.

I am not by nature the world's best housekeeper, even on my best days. But now dishes piled high in the sink, mail sat unopened on the table, and clothes littered my bedroom floor. Every day I woke up, went to work, and tried to concentrate, then went home and ate myself into oblivion or stared at the television until the wee hours. After about ten days of this, the phone rang. For some reason I still don't entirely understand, I answered instead of letting the answering machine pick up.

It was Donna. "I didn't see you in church last week, Heidi. Somebody told me your back was hurting. Do you need anything?"

"No."

"Do you want to get together for tea?"

"Not today."

Dead silence on the other end. Then, "OK, then. I'm coming over."

"No, wait, I—" But the line went dead. Nuts. Nuts. Nuts. As quickly as I could I shuffled around the room, kicking things under the couch and closing as many doors as possible to hide the grime.

The intercom buzzed ten minutes later. *How did she get here so fast?* I fumed, stuffing more dishes into the dishwasher. The kitchen reeked of rotten bananas. There was no hiding the truth. I went to the panel and flipped the "Talk" switch. "Yes?"

"C'mon, Heidi, let me in. I mean it."

I sighed and flipped the "open" switch.

Donna walked in and looked around without comment, then marched to my bedroom and flung open my door. "Oh,

Heidi…" Her voice was heavy with reproach.

"Oh, what?"

"You know what. Why didn't you *call* me? Now, you can drive, right? You need to get some fresh air. You will leave this minute—I don't care where. Go to the park, or go to the movies, or go to the library. Anywhere. You will not come back here, under any circumstances, for three hours."

I looked at my watch. It was three o'clock in the afternoon. "But—"

"No buts. Out. Now."

"But my back hurts!" I whined.

"You probably need a little exercise. Go on."

"I can't believe you're throwing me out of my own house."

"Believe it. Now go. See you at six."

Defeated, I snatched my purse from under a pile of newspapers and trudged outside. A bird was singing. Some kids were jumping in the leaves next door. The whole world had conspired to make me feel better in spite of myself.

Three hours later I returned to find a note on my front door. "Dinner's on the stove. Let me know if you can't find anything. Love, Donna." Inside, the place had been positively transformed. The drapes were open, letting light into all the corners of my living room. Newspapers were neatly stacked in a recycle bin. Dishes had been washed and put in cupboards. The clothes were off the bedroom floor, laundered, and neatly tucked into my dresser or hung in the closet. Donna had even scrubbed the shower curtain and tucked all my pens and pencils into mugs. Unbelievable.

Going to the stove, I lifted the lid and closed my eyes to take a deep whiff. Mmmm…. Fresh vegetable beef soup. And my favorite ice cream was in the freezer. I had just scooped up a bowl and taken it to the kitchen table when the phone rang again.

"Heidi?"

"Donna! I don't know what to say! Why did you do this?"

"I know what it's like to feel down. I thought you needed a little cheering up. Do you feel better?"

"Well … yes. Yes, I do. Thank you."

"No thanks necessary. Consider it payback for when you came to see me in the hospital. Now, eat some soup, then fix yourself a bubble bath and read a good book. Then go to bed and get a good night's sleep. People care about you. Especially me."

Human kindness, in whatever form it takes, is one of the strongest arguments that we are indeed made in the image of God. We care not because of some primeval impulse, but because from the beginning God made us to be as loving as he is. "How great is the love the Father has lavished on us, that we should be called children of God" (1 Jn 3:1). If we are receptive to that love, in whatever form it comes to us, its power begins to transform us from the inside out.

Many Christians waste a good deal of time and emotional energy arguing about whether someone who does not profess to be a Christian (or at least the same "kind" or to the same degree as those among whom the argument is being passed) can be truly loving. "We are all evil at heart," the argument goes, "so if someone who is not a Christian does something good, it must be for some selfish motive."

Must it? Or is it possible that maybe, just maybe, God has begun to work in the heart of that person, and he or she has begun to reflect—however imperfectly—the image of the One who loves him best? "Dear friends, let us love one another, for love comes from God. Everyone who loves has been born of God and knows God ... because God is love" (1 Jn 4:7-8).

Experiencing God's love from unlikely sources—as I did from the hands of my chronically depressed acquaintance—can be a startling revelation. When we show God's love to others, however, and it comes full circle to bless us back, we should not be surprised. If we are humble enough to receive these unexpected sources of grace, God is able to work through our "objects of ministry" in a way that will touch us profoundly and teach us lessons we will never forget.

In the seventh chapter of Luke, a "sinful woman" disrupts an elaborate dinner party at the home of one of the Pharisees, at which Jesus was an honored guest (see 7:36-47). The passage does not tell us precisely the nature of the woman's wrongdoing, but records her expressions of love for Jesus in vivid detail: she washes his feet with her tears, dries them with her own hair, kisses them, and breaks open a vial of expensive perfume so rich that, as it flows over the feet of the Lord, the aroma permeates the entire house.

Notice what happens next. The Pharisee dismisses not only the woman for ruining his dinner with her presence, but Jesus as well for not recognizing her impurity, for allowing her to touch him. Jesus, on the other hand, is deeply moved by the woman's actions, and uses the experience as a "teaching moment" to convey to all those present the wideness of God's mercy, the depths of his forgiveness to those who are truly repentant.

In the pages of this final section, you will encounter people whose actions prompted me to look hard at myself, to think about the way I was showing the love of Jesus to those around me. Their profession of faith may not have been perfectly formed, and yet each of them was a living object lesson. When this kind of insight hits us between the eyes, it forms a kind of "circle of love" that touches and transforms us in unimaginable ways. And when it happens, blessed is the person who is "child" enough to receive it gratefully.

—H.S.

Thirty-Two

Mrs. A. and the Razor

Compassion is a virtue that takes seriously the reality of other persons, their inner lives, their emotions, as well as their external circumstances. It is an active disposition toward fellowship and sharing, toward supportive companionship in distress or in woe.

WILLIAM BENNETT, *THE BOOK OF VIRTUES*

I never saw Peggy's mom make cookies, like other moms I knew. When we came home from school, Mrs. A. would always be on the couch, smoking a cigarette. She had a bad back that made it hard for her to get around. When Peggy joined our high-school Bible study group, we sometimes prayed for her mom.

From time to time I would chat with Mrs. A. while waiting for Peggy. Unsure that she was a Christian (she attended a different church than I did), I would try to help God along a bit by explaining how to know for sure she was going to heaven. Mrs. A. was always very nice, but firm. "Now, Heidi, go downstairs with Peg. I've got my church, and you have yours." I always did what she said. I knew better than to talk back to an adult.

The winter after I graduated from high school, I was in a bad car accident. Hospitalized and bedridden for over a month, I grew more and more depressed. Friends came by and brought cheery cards and flowers, but all I wanted was a shower. My hair was dirty and stringy, and I felt gross all over.

Then one morning the door to my room opened and in walked Mrs. A. I was surprised that Peggy's mother even knew I was in the hospital—I had been out of touch with her daughter since Peggy had left for college the previous fall. "Mrs. A.! What are you doing here?"

Smiling, Mrs. A. went into the bathroom and got a basin. Taking a garbage bag from her purse, she pushed back the covers from my bed and arranged the bag and the basin under my left shin. Then she squirted my leg with a can of shaving cream, rubbed it around, and carefully shaved me from my ankle to my knee, chatting all the while. It was glorious.

Pouring a little water into the basin, she swished the razor around to get rid of the hair, then bent over her task again. First one leg, then the other, chatting amiably the whole time. When she was done, she lowered the head of my bed and rigged another contraption so she could wash and blow dry my hair. Then, as a final touch, she painted my nails a cheery pink—fingers and toes. For the first time in a month, I felt like a human being. Admiring my newly pinked fingernails, I asked her, "What made you think of this, Mrs. A.?"

"Oh, I know what it feels like not to be able to reach your toes. I figured you might need a little help. That's what it's all about, right? 'Love one another.'"

A pang of guilt hit me. How could I have doubted that she loved God? Mrs. A. had shown me more kindness in a half-hour than I had shown her in two years. But she just brushed aside my apologies. "Here. Have a little ice cream." And from her magic bag she pulled out a pint of my favorite lemon sherbet— and soon the world was right again.

—*H.S.*

Thirty-Three

Long-Haired Lenny

While Jesus was having dinner at Matthew's house, many tax collectors and "sinners" came and ate with him and his disciples. When the Pharisees saw this, they asked his disciples, "Why does your teacher eat with tax collectors and 'sinners'?"

On hearing this, Jesus said, "It is not the healthy who need a doctor, but the sick. But go and learn what this means: 'I desire mercy, not sacrifice.' For I have not come to call the righteous, but sinners."

MATTHEW 9:10-13

Lenny was not exactly the kind of role model most parents wanted for their children. He was a Jesus Freak from the roots of his long, stringy hair to the soles of his sandaled feet. Strumming his guitar with overgrown thumbnails, I thought he looked like his best friend Jesus, of whom he talked incessantly.

We made an unlikely pair, Lenny and me. My wildest impulse up to that point had been to buy a Fleetwood Mac cassette. (Since rock-and-roll was strictly forbidden at our house, I didn't actually play the tape. I just squirreled it under my trundle bed as my own little declaration of independence.) Lenny, on the other hand, had led a life of colorful mystery that he now vaguely referred to as "my B.C. days."

The lack of detail intrigued me. I had lived a fairly sheltered existence up to that point, so from the few facts I knew of Lenny's past, I could sketch in the details in my mind only in the faintest pastels. My parents, on the other hand, took one look at Lenny and connected the dots in flaming Technicolor.

Wisely, my mother did not try to talk me out of the friendship. When his beat-up van pulled into the driveway, she would simply roll her eyes and disappear into the kitchen to make a pan of biscuits. The only thing Lenny did with more enthusiasm than talk about Jesus was eat my mother's cooking. Between mouthfuls of peanut butter biscuits and milk, Lenny talked animatedly about what God had done in his life, punctuating his stories liberally with Bible verses.

Lenny often spoke with a kind of wistful nostalgia about a place that sounded a bit like heaven on earth, a little Christian community and Bible school in Minneapolis called Bethany Fellowship. He encouraged me to think about going there. "You oughtta check it out, Heidi—you'd really like it." At which point my parents quickly changed the subject. They were not ready to send their eldest daughter to any school that would accept the likes of Lenny.

Less than a year later, my life was brought to an abrupt standstill when the car I was driving spun on a patch of ice and careened downhill into oncoming traffic. The only thing I remember about the first week was a dream in which my old Sunday school teacher, Mrs. Craig, appeared at the foot of my bed to have a little "heart to heart."

In my dream, she did not seem the least bit concerned about

the tubes and traction pulleys that crisscrossed my bed in that intensive care unit. Sternly she waggled a finger at me. "Heidi, it seems to me that God has had to do something pretty drastic to get your attention. You're being given a second chance. Don't waste it." And with that, I woke up. Days later I found out that I had nearly died in that accident. When I was well on the way to recovery, someone showed me a picture of the car I had been driving; it looked like a crumbled ball of blue tinfoil.

Over a month passed before I was released and brought home to the hospital bed my parents had set up in our dining room. It was six months before I was walking again. But during that time Lenny visited me often, and listened patiently as I worked through my questions about why God had allowed this to happen to me.

Thinking that I somehow needed to pay God back for sparing my life, I decided to become a missionary. I applied to Bethany College of Missions and was accepted there—because of the work-study program, the price was right, and I needed a change. I flew to Minneapolis with two suitcases containing all my worldly possessions.

When I arrived at Bethany, it was not exactly what I had expected based on Lenny's description of the place. It looked exactly like many other Christian colleges—not a longhaired, guitar totin' Jesus Freak in sight! As I got to know the staff, I occasionally dropped Lenny's name into the conversation, hoping that someone would remember him. Finally someone did.

"You're kidding. *You* know Lenny?"

I nodded.

"Well … he was…" The man paused again, clearing his throat. "An *unusual* student."

I smiled. "He spoke very highly of this place."

"You're kidding," he repeated in a flat monotone as I stood up to leave.

This experience was repeated on several occasions in the weeks and months that followed: the furrowed brow, the look of surprise, the choked "You're kidding" as one after another in the community remembered my favorite Jesus Freak. They had not thought him a conventional role model. Yet Lenny's kindness had made a big impression on me, and his example still encouraged me to break from my "safe" Christian boundaries and embrace the wild adventures God had in store for me.

"God chose the foolish things of the world to shame the wise; God chose the weak things of the world to shame the strong. He chose the lowly things of this world and the despised things ... so that no one may boast before him. It is because of him that you are in Christ Jesus, who has become for us wisdom from God—that is, our righteousness, holiness and redemption" (1 Cor 1:27-30).

—*H.S.*

The Missionary Lady

He is no fool who gives what he cannot keep
to gain what he can never lose.

JIM ELLIOT

W hen I was twenty-two, I was named Miss Florida and became a hometown celebrity. Shortly after, I was asked by a local Christian college to sing at a chapel service during a special week of meetings called "Women in Ministry."

That morning I spent a lot of time primping, as I was very concerned about how I looked: what I wore, how well my hair and makeup turned out....

Not bad, I concluded, rather self-satisfied, as I sat down after finishing my performance.

Then the speaker was introduced. A missionary in Africa for forty years, she was at least eighty years old. She shuffled to the podium wearing orthopedic shoes and a polyester suit, her hair combed into a neat bun. The first twenty years of her time in Africa had been spent ministering with her husband, but after his death, she had continued alone for another twenty years. She told of sick children she had nursed, students she had taught to read the Bible, and the many people she had led to the Lord.

The longer she spoke, the more I squirmed. I had been so preoccupied with my appearance, I had failed to be concerned about how I was communicating Jesus to this audience of women—which was the whole point of my being there! I couldn't have been more ashamed if there had been a neon sign over my head reading, "This is no woman in ministry. She is self-centered and full of pride."

As I thought about my heart attitude, I knew that I had to do a lot of maturing and changing if I ever wanted to become a woman of God. I was on the road to becoming a woman afraid to grow old, a woman who spent all of her time and money at a plastic surgeon's office. Was that how I wanted to end up? Certainly not!

That morning I prayed that God would change my heart. I wanted to be like this godly and grace-filled woman who had become more beautiful through the years because of her love for her Savior and everyone she met. I wanted to look back on my life someday and know that I had walked the path that led to wisdom.

I'm so thankful that God allowed me to see what was truly in my heart. He used this missionary in an unexpected way: not to tell someone in a foreign country about the love of Jesus, but to show an American beauty queen how to become a truly beautiful woman of God.

"Do not love the world or anything in the world. If anyone loves the world, the love of the Father is not in him. For everything in the world—the cravings of sinful man, the lust of his eye,s and the boasting of what he has and does—comes not from the Father but from the world. The world and its desires pass away, but the man who does the will of God lives forever" (1 Jn 2:15-17).

—*K.B*

Thirty-Five

Christmas Cadeau

Blessed are you who are poor,
for yours is the kingdom of God.
Blessed are you who hunger now,
for you will be satisfied.

LUKE 6:20-21a

The African sun baked the roof of my VW bug, forcing me to roll down the windows for a breath of fresh air. I had been in Dakar four months, and I knew what was coming. The moment I braked at a stoplight, beggars of every age and size swarmed my car, looking for a handout. *"Cadeau? Cadeau?"* They looked especially hopeful today, for Friday was the traditional Muslim almsgiving day. Wearily I smiled and pressed coins into a few hands, then stepped on the gas and turned into Supermarché. I wanted ice cream.

Entering the grocery store, I noticed a grubby Father Christmas hanging like a piñata from the light fixture. A wave of homesickness washed over me. Christmas in a Muslim country was not exactly the stuff carols are made of. The holiday was just a few days away, and I was determined to make the best of it. But how?

As I stood there in the air-conditioned supermarket, inspiration struck. I grabbed a bag of oranges, paid for them, and headed for the street. Smiley Charlie was sitting on his mat near the baobab tree just outside the store, his useless right leg tucked underneath him. He was always in the same spot because his leprosy made movement difficult. Charlie waved and smiled as he saw me approach. *"Cadeau, Mademoiselle?"*

I had a gift for him, all right. Opening the sack of fruit, I held up one of the orange-and-brown-speckled orbs. His eyes widened with surprise. Seeing that his gnarled hands would be unable to peel the fruit, I did it for him. Then I placed one of the segments in his mouth and put the rest in his outstretched palm. He closed his eyes, chewing slowly, savoring the flavor.

A high-pitched giggle ruffled the air behind me, then another. Turning, I saw a couple of urchins eyeing my sack. I reached into the bag and held an orange out to them; the closest boy snatched it from my hands and bit down without bothering to remove the rind. Three more children ran up, and I started handing out fruit as fast as I could. In no time I had incited a small riot as adults and children alike pushed, pulled, groped, and clawed their way toward me, each intent on claiming their golden bit of heaven. In seconds the entire bag was empty.

Slowly the crowd dispersed. Some held their prize aloft and chortled gleefully, others gobbled the fruit and licked their fingers. Those who had not been fast enough shrugged and returned to their respective posts along the street, waiting for another car to stop at the street light. Already I could hear the voices entreating, *"Cadeau? Cadeau?"*

That night as I was writing in my journal, I pondered the events of that day. Such excitement over a bag of oranges! At home the oranges would have to have been dipped in gold to get a response like the one I got that day! And yet... Wasn't this a kind of poverty too? In a sense, these poor beggars were richer than I was—they knew how to revel in the simplest abundance.

—H.S.

Thirty-Six

The Muslim Missionary

Surely, when the Day of Judgment comes, we shall not be asked what we have read but what we have done, not how well we have spoken but how devoutly we have lived.

THOMAS À KEMPIS

During my second year of Bible college, a group of us would gather several nights a week in a certain lounge after study hours were over. Drinking tea and arguing tirelessly, we were highly confident that God had given us the inside scoop, settling once and for all questions that had plagued theologians for centuries. So convinced were we of our own intellectual and spiritual prowess, it never occurred to us that there still might be a few things we needed to learn about who God is and how he operates.

In short, we were insufferable.

Perhaps for this reason, the school had designated the third year of its program to be a practical year of service. Time to put aside our neat little theological boxes, leap out in faith, and trust God to catch us. And so, here I was in Senegal. On this particular day I was seated on the steps of the post office, fanning myself and waiting for a co-worker to finish buying stamps.

Suddenly a man stood before me. He was Mauritanian; his characteristic white headgear encircled his face, drawing my attention to his deep-set yet kindly eyes. He said something to me, pointing emphatically skyward. I did not understand what he was saying, but I had heard the tone often enough to understand his intent. He was a Muslim street evangelist. I smiled and shook my head. *"Je m'escuse, Monsieur. Je ne comprends pas."*

He stepped back, momentarily baffled. Then he did what most people do when they encounter someone who does not speak their language—he repeated himself at half the speed and twice the volume. When my friend emerged from the post office, he launched into his message again, this time gesturing at both of us. "He wants to know if we believe in Allah," she explained to me. Softly she told him with equal earnestness of her friend, Jesus.

The man seemed to anticipate her response. He smiled, showing great white teeth, and engaged my friend in dialogue for nearly twenty minutes, explaining why Allah was the only true God, and Mohammed the greatest of the prophets. He was not angry—if anything, he seemed sorry that we were not persuaded by his arguments. Finally he turned on his heel and left us in peace.

I thought about that encounter for the rest of the day. Here was a man who believed as vehemently about his faith as I did about mine. From what I could tell (and my friend later confirmed this), he had a well-reasoned and polite response for every question we put to him. But we could not shake his faith any more than he was able to shake ours—instead we reached something of a spiritual impasse.

This was the first time I had encountered a non-Christian who had such a systematic understanding of his faith. It had never occurred to me that someone wouldn't "see the light" through simple rhetoric. But I had been raised in the rolling hills of the Bible Belt; everyone I knew was a Christian, at least on paper. The man I met that day had been raised in a culture where the vast majority of people were Muslim.

Despite our differences in culture and creed, we had much in common. We both "knew" with absolute certainty that ours was the only real way to God and shared our faith with anyone who would listen. Both of us proselytized with benevolent intentions: to spare those who did not see things as we did from the fiery torments of hell.

Even if I could have spoken his language, how on earth would I ever be able to reach someone like this man for Christ? Someone who was able to deflate or deflect every question or argument I could raise? For the first time since I had entered Bible school, I had more questions than answers. I had gotten A's in hermeneutics and linguistics, but in that moment I realized just how clueless I was when it came to showing someone the love of Christ.

That day I learned an important lesson. Evangelism at its best involves more than poking holes in another person's worldview or spouting the right combination of Bible verses. Intellectual converts are few and far between. Christianity is, first and foremost, about relationship. It is about feeding souls made hungry by the Spirit with the pure, sweet nectar of faith. In the words of Augustine, "Preach the Gospel. When necessary, use words."

—H.S.

Thirty-Seven

The Milk of Human Kindness

A man of many companions may come to ruin,
but there is a friend who sticks closer than a brother.

PROVERBS 18:24

My husband, Gary, had the privilege of singing in the recording studio for two sessions for Bill and Gloria Gaither's Homecoming video series. He sang with gospel greats such as Jake Hess, Ann Downing, Rex Nelon, Ben Speer, and many others. During a break in one of the sessions, Bill Gaither shared a recent experience that had touched him deeply.

Long before Bill and Gloria Gaither became household names for their talent as gospel singers, they were schoolteachers, and lived next door to a very large family. Neither the Gaithers nor their neighbors had any disposable income. They were all struggling to make ends meet.

In spite of their own financial situation, Bill and Gloria felt compelled to pay their neighbor's milk bill. The Gaithers knew that a family with several young children needed the nutritional value milk would provide, so they volunteered to take on this added expense.

This went on for many years, until, as so often happens, both families moved and eventually lost touch with each other. As Bill recounted the story in the studio, he said he never thought much more about the milk money.

Then one day, a young man walked up to him. "Mr. Gaither," he said, "you don't know me and you may not even remember my family, but I was one of the children whose milk you bought when we were neighbors. I just wanted to say thank you, and let you know that my family has always been grateful for what you and Mrs. Gaither did for us years ago."

As Bill and the young man talked, Bill learned that the children in the family were now adults who had gone to college, had successful careers, and were raising families of their own.

It's hard to say what impact that milk had in the lives of these children. No doubt their mom and dad were grateful to know that no matter what, their kids would have milk to drink that day. Maybe the children learned a valuable lesson about the importance of reaching out to those in need. Maybe they in turn are touching their neighbors through their generosity because someone provided an example of compassion during the early stages of their lives.

God's great circle of love—spilling into our lives until we can't help but pass it along to others—has a way of multiplying. Each human act of love, done in the name of Jesus, blesses not only those who receive it but those who give it as well. Years later, the same love for God that prompted the Gaithers' act of kindness for that needy family was multiplied in their own lives—and spilled over into the lives of millions of others as those two schoolteachers became legends in gospel music.

—K.B.

Thirty-Eight

Katherine

Take a chance! All life is a chance. The man who goes furthest is generally the one who is willing to do and dare.

DALE CARNEGIE

I barely caught my connection in New York, boarding the plane to Dakar just moments before the flight attendants closed the door. I was going to spend a year in West Africa, teaching at Dakar Academy as a short-term missionary. I wasn't sure what to expect when I got there, but I was ready for an adventure.

When I found my seat on the plane, a young woman with dark hair and wire-rimmed glasses had occupied the window seat next to mine. Katherine was a graduate student on her way to Dakar to study the textile industry. Having discovered on the previous flight how the word "missionary" put people off, I told Katherine only that I was going to be an English teacher at a school in the city.

"Where in the city is the school?" Katherine asked.

"Umm … actually, I'm not sure," I confessed.

She looked at me strangely. "You don't know where you're going? How will you get there?"

"Someone is going to meet my plane," I answered. She nodded absently, then pushed her nightshades over her eyes and leaned back in her chair.

The man seated across the aisle smiled at me. His dark skin made his white cotton shirt look even brighter, and his expensive gold wristwatch sparkled. Near the end of the trip he said something to me in French, but as I had not yet cracked open my French language tapes, my only response was an apologetic shrug.

Soon our plane had landed. I looked out my window and saw nothing but a few palm trees and several scrawny cats. At least, I hoped they were cats. The hot African sun beat on the tarmac, and we all hustled inside for a bit of shade. When it was my turn with the customs agent, he asked me something I did not understand. I responded with the only French I knew: *"Parlez anglaise, monsieur?"*

"Of course he doesn't speak English. You're in Senegal, not London," Katherine's voice broke in just behind me. Gratefully, I smiled. She said a few words to the agent, who waved us through.

"Are your people here?" my new friend questioned me. Frankly, I had no idea. Ours were the only white faces in the airport, so it wouldn't have been too difficult for my contact to figure out who I was. But as the minutes ticked by, it was clear that no one had come to meet my plane.

"Let's try the phone book," Katherine suggested. "What's the name of the school?"

My mind went blank. I had neglected to write it down. "I'm

not sure…" my voice trailed off.

She rolled her eyes. "You don't know who's meeting you, you don't know the name of the school. Is there anything you *do* know?"

I felt truly foolish.

"Never mind," Katherine answered her own question. "Okay, we'll take a taxi around the area. Sooner or later, we're bound to run into a missionary. Heaven knows they're easy to spot. White skin and no fashion sense." She chuckled at her own joke.

We were nearly at the airport entrance. "Hold on to your bags, now, Heidi," Katherine admonished me. "These porters survive on tips." No sooner had the words left her mouth than my suitcases disappeared from my arms. I turned to see Katherine beating off one of the porters with her carry-on. Five men were running with my luggage to the nearest taxi.

"Do you have any small change?" Katherine asked me. I didn't. Ten hands—two from each porter—reached in through my taxi window. Not knowing what else to do, I rolled up the window. This did not please the taxi driver, who doubled the fare he originally quoted us.

It was only the beginning of a very long afternoon driving through the streets of downtown Dakar. Fortunately, we did spot a missionary who knew the director of the school where I would be teaching. Together we drove to *La Phare de l'Esperance* (Beacon of Hope), a magnificent lighthouse on the city's coastline. Getting out of the taxi, I unloaded my bags and gratefully waved good-bye to Katherine, with whom I made plans for dinner later in the week.

Later in the day, I found out that the missionary who was

supposed to have met my plane had not received the message from headquarters until long after Katherine and I had started our taxi ride. As I climbed into bed that night, I remember feeling secure in the knowledge that when human plans had failed, God had provided a place of safety for me through the kindness of a stranger.

—H.S.

Thirty-Nine

Bus Ride to Heaven

*Reflect on your present blessings of which every man has many,
not on your past misfortunes of which all men have some.*

CHARLES DICKENS

After being on the road for over a month, we prepared to cross over from Poland into Germany, where we would receive the concert schedule for the rest of our tour. Four of our team members had miraculously received their visas at the last possible moment, and we felt sure that God was guiding us into our next adventure. But by the time we reached the German border, we were exhausted.

Unfortunately, our German itinerary had a few holes. We had accommodations for only a few nights, so the rest of the time we had to "wing it." And since we had lost both our translator and our chaplain, the team began to question whether it was God or our own stubbornness that had brought us to Germany.

The mood grew darker with every mile. None of our Polish friends had been in a Western country before—the Iron Curtain had shielded them from the dark side of capitalism. But now as we rode through Berlin, the Poles looked with horror at billboards and other advertisements that lined the streets. "This is bad!" Jan exclaimed, rifling through his Polish-English dictionary in an effort to find the word that expressed his dismay. I looked to where his finger was pointing: *pornography.*

"Why we come here?!" one of the others demanded. "Everything is ... dirty."

"God brought us here. Remember the passports?" I tried to be encouraging, but by this time I was wondering the same thing. *God, what were you thinking?*

The three hundred dollars I had been given at the beginning of the trip "for emergencies" was quickly disappearing— German *marks* were far more expensive than Polish *złøty.* We stopped a few times, held impromptu outdoor concerts, and managed to find places to sleep and eat on those days we had no concerts scheduled. Then, three days before the trip was over, we took a wrong turn and wound up in the middle of nowhere, with no idea what to do next.

I asked the bus driver to stop near a small clearing, and gathered the group around. "We don't have much money left, not nearly enough for the next three days. I need everyone to give what they can, to get us through." A hat was passed, but in the end we had gathered just under $20.

I was desperate. *God, you wouldn't leave us out here like this. Where should we go? What should we do?* We must have sat there for the better part of an hour, praying as hard as we could for revelation.

God's answer arrived in a tin can on wheels—a low-budget German car. Inside were an old man and woman who had stopped to see if we needed assistance. With the bus driver's help I explained our situation as best I could, and the old man said simply, "Come, follow us."

Not knowing what else to do, we piled back on the bus and followed them down miles of winding country roads. At last the old man turned on his right blinker, pointed to a large structure just ahead—and vanished around a corner.

We drove up to the compound and I went inside. It was a large Christian conference center. Hearing our plight, the director of the conference center suggested that we stay a few days until it was time for us to leave for our next concert. Gladly, we accepted.

After eating and relaxing a bit, all of us were in a much better frame of mind to finish the trip. We had been asked to provide music for the evening meeting at the conference center, which we were glad to do.

We had just finished our last song when the director came up to me. "Will you say a few words to us?"

"My German is not very good," I hedged.

"We have someone who will translate for you," she replied.

My mind in a whirl, I stood before what looked like a thousand people, though it was really not more than a few hundred. At last a coherent thought came to me.

"Thank you, friends, for allowing us to stay with you these past few days. Your kindness is appreciated more than you can imagine.

"As we prepare to return to our homes, I have been thinking of the reasons God brought this team together, and of what we have learned from the experience.

"More than anything, the lesson can be summed up in one sentence: *'Wie gross ist dein Gott?'* How big is your God? Every time we made plans, God laughed and sent us another way. And every time, he has been faithful to give us what we needed for this new adventure.

"What we experienced this summer is not so different from what all of us experience every day of our lives. Each day we are given the opportunity to trust God, to leave in his great hands the smallest concerns of our hearts. By these little acts of faith we are blessed, for when we release our plans to him, God demonstrates that he has much better things in mind for us.

"So I ask you now, *'Wie gross ist dein Gott?'* Is he someone so small that he can be easily contained in a church? Or great and loving enough to be trusted with the deepest concerns of our hearts?"

—*H.S.*

Forty

"Well Done, Good and Faithful Servants"

"Be faithful, even to the point of death, and I will give you the crown of life."

In the Gospel of Matthew, Jesus tells a parable that I have always found particularly puzzling. It's the story of a man who owned a great vineyard and who went to the marketplace to find day laborers to pick his crops (see Mt 20:1-16).

Early in the morning, the landowner sees a group of men in the village square and hires them to work for him that day at the going rate—a denarius. They agree and start picking grapes.

A few hours later, the man decides the grapes aren't piling up in those baskets fast enough, and he goes out to hire a few more men. When he finds them, he tells them to go to work, and that he will pay them "whatever is right" (vs. 4). The vineyard owner does this again three hours later, and again towards the end of the day.

I always wondered about that last bunch. Had they simply arrived at the market square later than the others? I could sympathize with that, not being a morning person myself.

Or were they somehow less desirable workers? Had they recognized the man's invitation to work as gentle charity? As they hoisted those baskets piled high with produce, were they grateful that at least this night their children would not go hungry? Of course, they had worked only an hour.... But maybe, if they worked hard enough, there would be money enough for at least a mouthful of bread for them all.

Imagine, then, their open-mouthed delight when the money-bag was opened and those ninth-hour laborers saw that flash of silver. A whole day's wage! They could not believe their good fortune, the best thing that had happened to them for as long as they could remember.

Every time I read this story, I am reminded that God does not measure the value or completeness of a task with the same standard that we do. Some of his servants toil for fifty or sixty years. The life's work of others may be of a much shorter duration.

Ken and Anna Peterson were a young missionary couple that I met while teaching at Dakar Academy in Senegal, West Africa. They had just graduated from French language school and were eager to begin their first term of full-time missionary service. Their three children attended the Academy, and so between Wolof language lessons (the predominant dialect in that area), Ken made himself useful at the school. He and another teacher instituted a long-distance running program with the junior-high boys, and frequently took packs of kids running in the park across the street from the school.

Before he finished his first year, Ken was out running in the park with his son when he dropped dead of a heart attack. He was young, and had apparently been in perfect health. No one could understand how something like this could happen. Didn't God realize that Ken's work had just begun?

This past spring I experienced the same rush of painful surprise. A young man I had known at Bible school, Paul Atkins, had been serving in Albania with his wife and small children. His doctors had discovered a small heart murmur and fit Paul with a pacemaker, and in time gave him medical clearance to return to his post. A few days later, Paul collapsed in his wife's arms and died. He was just thirty-four.

Both these men were in the prime of life. Both burned with an inner zeal to serve the Lord with all their mind and strength. Both left behind small children and grieving widows. Both, by all appearances, had barely scratched the surface of the work God had called them to do before they were suddenly pulled from their "fields" to receive their final reward.

I do not pretend to understand why God allowed these things to happen. It seems monumentally unfair—after all, it's not as if God has more career missionaries than he can handle. But maybe that puzzling parable from Matthew's gospel holds the key. Whether we labor one hour or ten, we can trust the Great Keeper of the Vines to reward us when the time is right.

—*H.S.*

To honor the memory of Paul Atkins, Bethany Fellowship International has begun the Paul Atkins Fund to promote the main aspects of Paul's ministry, which were evangelism and church planting. Donations are tax deductible, and all donors will receive periodic updates of how their donations are changing

families and communities with the good news of Jesus Christ. For
more information, call or write Bethany Fellowship International:

Bethany Fellowship International
6820 Auto Club Road
Minneapolis, MN 55438
612-996-1382
www.bethfel.org

Conclusion

I have a confession. When it comes to kindness, I am far more likely to be on the receiving end than the giving end. For this reason, I am reluctant to call attention to any small act of kindness on my part.

However, my husband Craig, who is the kindest person I know, asked me to write a story about our "children," two border collies named Missy and Dogbert. So I would like to tell you one final story of how a bit of human kindness can bring unimaginable blessing—whether the object of that love has two feet or four.

I raised Missy from a pup. For the first nine months of her life, it was just the two of us in a big old rambling farmhouse in northeast Ann Arbor. It quickly became apparent that she was an unusually bright animal, and more than a little strong-willed. (Some might say "spoiled," but not in my presence!) She chased cows by day and kept me company at night. It was a cozy arrangement.

When Craig came along, she tested his mettle by making him fish her favorite pink ball out of a lake and prancing circles around him, daring him to chase her into the house when it was time to come in for supper.* (Craig was smart enough not to take the second challenge—he is every bit as smart as Missy, but not nearly as fast.)

* For the unabridged version of this story, check out "Love in the Park," published by Broadman & Holman in *Heart-Stirring Stories of Romance*.

Then we got married, Craig and I. And we decided to get another border collie. When the Border Collie Rescue lady first showed us Sampson (we renamed him Dogbert—my husband is a "Dilbert" fan), we very nearly didn't take him. He was skin and bones, and his eyes were sunk deep into the back of his head. In addition, his unusually strong herding instinct induced him to run circles around—and nip the heels of—anything that moved.

Dogbert had been badly treated, and it showed. As a safety measure, we had him put through obedience training before we brought him home.

Once he came to live with us, the games began. Dogbert nipped my brother-in-law and snarled at our pastor. He chewed my favorite shoes and committed indiscretions whenever we left him alone in a room for five minutes.

But he also came when we called—which was more than we could say for Missy. And if we reproached him, he would cower and lick us compulsively until he was forgiven.

The days passed, and Dogbert began to relax. The fear-biting stopped, and he learned to return a Frisbee when we tossed it to him—instead of flinging it in the air and catching it himself in a weird kind of "Frisbee solitaire." After a month, his ribs no longer showed, and he stopped draining his water dish every time we filled it. (We tried not to think about how often he had been left outside with neither food nor water.) The crazy look in his eyes disappeared.

Now, apart from the occasional bout of sibling rivalry between Dogbert and Missy, we are one big happy family. It's amazing what a little love will do.

This world in which we live is full of Missys and Dogberts.

The Missys are easy to spot—we are sleek and sassy, full of the confidence that comes from knowing that the Master loves us. We have never gone to bed hungry and are possibly just the slightest bit spoiled.

Then there are the Dogberts. The love-starved, wild-eyed, snarling bits of humanity that are desperately in need of a compassionate touch of kindness. You know the ones I'm talking about: the rotten kid in your Sunday school class, that freeloading relative who makes every holiday a misery, the bickering couple next door.

The next time you encounter your own personal Dogbert, commit yourself to bringing God's love full-circle. You're not sure how? In the Gospel of Matthew, Jesus used his own four-footed metaphor—sheep and goats instead of border collies—to show us exactly how. Listen as he speaks to your heart again:

When the Son of Man comes in his glory, and all the angels with him, he will sit on his throne in heavenly glory. All the nations will be gathered before him, and he will separate the people one from another as a shepherd separates the sheep from the goats. He will put the sheep on his right and the goats on his left.

Then the King will say to those on his right, "Come, you who are blessed by my Father; take your inheritance, the kingdom prepared for you since the creation of the world. For I was hungry and you gave me something to eat, I was thirsty and you gave me something to drink, I was a stranger and you invited me in, I needed clothes and you clothed me, I was sick and you looked after me, I was in prison and you came to visit me."

Then the righteous will answer him, "Lord, when did we see you hungry and feed you, or thirsty and give you something to drink? When did we see you a stranger and invite you in, or needing clothes and clothe you? When did we see you sick or in prison and go to visit you?"

The King will reply, "I tell you the truth, whatever you did for one of the least of these brothers of mine, you did for me."

MATTHEW 25:31-40

Each of us has been touched by God's kindness, has been given the power to make a difference in our corner of the world. To the degree that we respond to that call to care, we reflect in a small way the life-giving community of the Trinity. To the extent that we reflect the compassion of our Lord, looking past appearances to love the person inside, we bring a small part of the kingdom of God into the here and now.

It is our prayer that the stories in this book will fortify you for your own journey of faith and encourage you to step outside your safety zone. Jesus has called us to love.

Let us begin the adventure today.

—H.S.

Acknowledgments

Although we—Heidi and Kim—were the ones who committed pen to paper and recorded these narratives, we could not have written this book alone. In many cases, the people whose stories we have told never imagined that their actions would become public knowledge. To protect their privacy, many of their names and some details have been changed. However, we do thank each of you. You know who you are.

Special thanks go to Andy Chrisman, Bob Carlisle, Joyce Martin McCollough, Heather Payne, Bill and Gloria Gaither, and Mark Lowry for volunteering to participate in this project. Because of them, many worthwhile charities will get the added exposure they need to continue their important work. Thanks, too, to those in leadership within these organizations, including Rory Starkes, Paul Moore, Pastor Phil Greenaway, and Carrie Abbot—both for participating in these interviews and for the work you are doing to help people all over the world.

I (Heidi) also offer special thanks to the people of Lafayette Federated Church in Lafayette, New Jersey. It was from them that I first learned what it meant to be Jesus' hands and feet to the world. I also want to thank my friends at Bethany Fellowship International (particularly Mike and Karen Leeming); United World Missions (especially Gene and Sheryl Toombs); Dawn and Frank Ponnett and Monsignor Connelly at Holy Family Parish in South Pasadena, California; and Father Roger Prokop and my other friends at St. Thomas the Apostle Church in Ann Arbor, Michigan. Our editor, Liz Heaney, is also to be commended, for she taught me how to be a better writer and editor through her involvement in this project.

My family and friends also played a vital part in the creation of this book—especially my husband, Craig. When in recent months "being like Jesus" seemed an impossible standard, I simply tried to emulate my husband's patience and kindness. Thanks, honey.

I (Kim) would especially like to thank Heidi for carrying more than her fair share of the writing of this book. You have been wonderful to work with, and I hope we can do it again.

And to my "men," Gary, Gar-Gar, and Alexander, thank you for being supportive of my work and ministry. I love you all very much.

Finally, thanks to everyone at Servant Publications who gave us a chance to put these stories in print, including Don Cooper and Bert Ghezzi.

—*Heidi Saxton and Kim Boyce*

Do you have a kindness story you would like to share? You can get in touch with us through the publisher. Or you can reach Heidi through her web site:
www.christianword.com
hsaxton@christianword.com

You can reach Kim at:
P.O. Box 1221
Hollister, MO 65673
Kim Boyce2@aol.com